HOLD YOUR OWN IN CONVERSATION

— with the joy of feeling at ease

D1476772

HOLD YOUR OWN IN CONVERSATION

— with the joy of feeling at ease

by
Elliot Russell

PAPERFRONTS

ELLIOT RIGHT WAY BOOKS
KINGSWOOD, SURREY, U.K.

Formerly titled The Conversation Secret
© Elliot Right Way Books MCMLIV
2nd Edition MCMLXV
© Revised, re-written and re-titled MCMLXXVII

Made and Printed in England
by Cox & Wyman Ltd., London, Reading and Fakenham

CONTENTS

Contents

Contents

INTRODUCTION

There are two main kinds of conversation, that interesting and often exciting on-going talk of accomplished conversationalists, into one of whom it will be my aim to develop you – and what is called small-talk or introductory conversation which breaks the ice.

This latter is important, particularly for people who happen to be shy, and I will try to show how to accomplish it by giving hints and examples. Without small talk the road to greater things is partially closed.

In an age of TV, Bingo and ever-increasing commercial exploitation of our leisure time we are in danger of losing the art of talk and with it much more. For, through conversation, we find and keep friends. In time artificial entertainments bore and weary us; true companions, however, to whom we can talk without second thought, are never dull.

Conversation is the human attribute – no animal can talk or laugh. If we are unable to indulge freely in it we may miss more than half of the pleasure of life. Can anybody afford that?

For people inexperienced in the science of good conversation, joining a lively bunch of friends for an evening can seem like an endurance test. Increasing self-conscious awareness that they are not contributing to the evening's fun as the party goes on, makes them begin to wish 'if *only* I could disappear!' Such strong fears taken too far can lead erroneously to the person becoming a social hermit who refuses invitations and soon gets forgotten and left out. To rationalize they may even kid themselves their own company is the best! (as they are happiest in it).

Oh what these folk miss; when all that is needed is to pick up and practise a few simple tricks of the trade!

If this book can release just a few such personalities it will have served its purpose. I hope that anyone who applies and improves on the ideas in this book will find how to Hold Their Own In Conversation – with the joy of feeling at ease.

1

BREAKING THE ICE

Before you can become a conversationalist in any company, you must know enough ways to break into that company, that is, unless you are properly introduced.

People often omit to introduce; either they forget, or perhaps *they* are afraid to butt in on assembled company. It may be they lack enough self-confidence to nip in and express their desire for you to be included – at a suitable conversational pause – or they may be worried that you might not like, or be liked, by the company.

Possibly more feeble is the half-hearted introduction so often an embarrassment to all. Contrast the empty 'George, meet Katelyn – Katelyn meet George' with a spry 'Hey! George *I want you* to meet Katelyn; she's come all the way from Bristol – Katelyn *I'd love you* to know George; we've known each other since we were boys!' Note how each can feel 'ten feet tall' and two possible subjects have been unobtrusively suggested for them – home background and mutual acquaintance. The introducer can now retire to attend to other guests or not, as he wishes.

As this book is not written for experts I make no apology for being elementary in this chapter. My hope is that shy people will find knowledge which is useful.

Many people fail to find friends or conversation because their small-talk is defective. Such people it seems are not born with an 'easy manner'. However, to break the ice in aeroplanes, sports clubs or when you like is not simple for

11

everyone, because, like many important things in life, we are not taught how in school. Yet what is more delightful than to be able to talk and possibly become friends with those whom you like the look of? Let's be honest about it! Hasn't everyone seen people at the races or sat next to someone in a train to whom we would like to have spoken but felt we dare not? Convention, etiquette, fear, or what you will have stood in the way. How *do* people successfully introduce themselves to strangers?

It's an art, make no mistake about that. It's an art in which the Americans are ahead of the British, from whom the latter can learn. But even in the United States there are shy people who miss golden opportunities.

The humbug of the whole thing perhaps begins when we are warned as children 'Don't speak to strangers'. This appropriate wise advice to children has a nasty habit of remaining in the way long after it has been outgrown.

The girl who tries to 'get off' at the beach by dropping her hanky may be suspect, but wherever there are young men and girls some way will be found of meeting – and many good friendships have been made unconventionally.

The classic (and true) example of the English nobleman who, seeing a pretty girl on the platform as the train passed, pulled the communication cord and eventually married her is only an exaggerated example of an acceptable long shot which worked!

Most of us judge people on sight; sometimes, although I believe less often than one might think, wrongly. However, owing to the unwritten laws of good manners, theoretically we can do nothing about it when we see someone we like. Fortunately, in practice, there is a great deal you can do.

SMALL TALK

The key, whether you wish to speak to the person waiting with you to be served in the shop or whether you want to introduce conversation to a bored and silent company on a holiday coach, is small talk.

This requires thought. Subjects such as the weather, apart from being trite, are apt to put people off. A little harmless subtlety is excusable if the ends justify the means! The art of small talk or introductory conversation can be improved by reading the gossip columns in the daily and weekly papers and magazines. By memorizing just surprisingly few interesting facts and information about people and things, you build up a store on which to draw. Especially if these 'facts' can appeal to people's sense of fun will they be good conversational sources. Fun makes the World go round!

In practice, opening a conversation requires experience, and at first you may fail miserably. You may even be snubbed, but don't worry over that because in time you will learn how to handle many differing occasions and types of people. Being snubbed may be no fault of yours. We are all gruff at times and you may just have come upon someone who, on that day at least, simply was rude. It is not easy to formulate rules because few situations are similar.

This may be said, however. Always be polite, diplomatic and careful not to offend. Always be able to retreat if you get the wrong reaction. Always try to find some topical way of starting as this stands a better chance. Be an opportunist.

To illustrate the last point, in the case of the proverbial railway carriage conversation (or lack of it) something usually happens which provides an opening for the skilful negotiator. It's quite simple when the train stops between stations. You can break silence with an 'excuse me' as you move to look out the window. The crack in the ice made by this remark makes it easier to break through entirely. When you tell the other passengers you 'can't see a thing' or that 'the 3.15 is just ahead' they will happily accept it. You could lead on by asking if anyone objects to the window being left open. From this point various openings can be made. Others are likely to talk back or, at this stage, even a popular TV show or sport will not seem out of place if you can't think of anything more exciting.

I purposely give a simple, almost strained, illustration. In many situations these straightforward methods are by far the best. This applies especially between the same sex. A man can ask another man in the golf club for a game without a thought. At tennis clubs mixed players can politely invite each other for a game, when there are four players. Anglers by the riverside invariably chat about their sport or the lack of it.

Even between opposite sexes, much can be done, provided it is nicely done, at the right time, in the right way and to the right person.

The middle-aged 'married-looking' man who tries to 'get off' with the attractive girl in a restaurant deserves what trouble he gets, if any. The young man, even were he simply to use the suspect 'Could you please tell me the correct time?' (suspect because it's as old as the hills as a method of trying to get acquainted) might get away with it, if the girl liked the look of him.

Better methods can be thought out, depending on the situation. A kindly offer of a menu or cruet, an appropriate remark about an accident to crockery, or even a well-timed and skilfully executed lifting of the eyebrows as some odd-looking fellow diner leaves might (or might not) all serve as a means of introduction.

Both men and women need to be careful, in dealing with strangers of the opposite sex, not to fall foul of mixing their own motives. Frank open conversational ploys, seeking only the mutually agreeable goal of companionship of the moment are rarely rebuffed. Out of place sexual desires even though perhaps unspoken will be 'sniffed' at once by the opposite number and are likely to cause instant conversation-stifling resentment. Having any such feelings properly in their place incidentally, leads to much happier encounters through life by eliminating unjustifiable disappointments.

I remember some years ago a very attractive girl asked a man the way to a station. He explained she could either go directly, which she would have to, if she wanted to catch her train, or in a roundabout way if she was content to go on the evening train. They had an enjoyable day. Where there's a will, as we say in Scotland, there's a way!

Difficult as is the meeting of strangers, even more difficult is the continuing of a conversation for many people after they have been introduced. Introduction, after all, doth not make a good companion. It certainly does not make a conversation. With people you don't know, conversation can be extremely trying unless you work to some sort of plan.

God preserve us from planned conversation, however! Most of this book is written especially to help avoid that and instead to show you how you can develop natural conversation which is enjoyable, interesting and spontaneous – how you can talk from the heart and mind.

All the same, the very shy and inexperienced will benefit if they can construct for themselves some sort of life-saving list of subjects to work on when the weather, the latest film and so on have served their purpose in the first few minutes.

This list can largely be discarded when you have really become a conversationalist proper – but till then it can be useful.

1. *Humorous happenings to yourself.* People like to hear these tales and often help the conversation by telling their own.

2. *The Narrow Escape Story.* Here is another favourite. Most of us have had some exciting experience which for the story's sake we can perhaps slightly exaggerate, but be very careful how you go because in company there is sometimes a stickler for hard facts who will pull you right up. I am reminded of a motorist who boasted of when he skidded and the car turned right round four times. I happened to feel sure this is all but impossible but kept silent. After all, his story was good and told for our benefit.

3. *Funny stories.* As I explain later it is best only to introduce amusing subjects which are appropriate to the time, place and company, but in desperate silences desperate remedies can be tried . . . with care.

4. *Confidences.* In trusted company, personal experiences are not only permissible but acceptable. They form topics which can provide almost endless conversation, but of course you must remember the larger the company the greater the risk of the confidence not being respected. With two people the risk is less but a secret once told, by definition, becomes thereafter a confidence. This fact may itself serve as a useful conversational topic!

5. *Character Reading.* This takes a lot of practice and experience but if skilfully done can provide great amusement. As with confidences care is required – remember the law of slander! And don't forget either that some people are sensitive. In the right company fun may be had by all whether character is read from the lines of the face, the

hands or tea-cups. Plenty of books are available from which to learn the basics of such character reading.

6. *Sex, Religion and Politics*. The age-old armed services tradition has it that these three subjects should be taboo in polite company, so much so that the idea is firmly embedded in social etiquette. Actually you need fear the subjects only in so far as they are *definitely not* good conversational starters with strangers. With people you know well they can in practice take their proper place as important areas of conversational focus – with care not to be adamant or simply argumentative. In reality in the Services, sex is one of the commonest subjects, garnished as you might expect with a sense of fun and perhaps a little innocent friendly ribbing between close chums!

7. *Health*. This can be boring especially if it's about your own health, but if you can contribute something showing the courage of another it often makes a good topic.

8. '*Shop*.' Another subject which is apt to bore but like the weather is probably one of the most common subjects spoken about. Discussing your job, in an interesting way, can be a good topic.

9. *Holidays you've had*. Another subject normally overworked but if the holiday has involved travel there is lots of hope. It depends what you have seen and done and maybe can recommend. As most people go for holidays it is a fertile subject for others to contribute to.

10. *Families*. Parents find much in common in discussing children. In other family affairs much care is needed not to divulge family secrets but simple questions about the size of the family, where the different members live and so on do form ice-breaking topics. One point here is that it is not regarded as polite to ask a person what is their trade or profession.

11. *Hobbies, Sport, Pastimes*. These are good stand-bys provided a proper angle of approach is used. It is useless to talk the language of the rugger man to someone who never played the game. But often a lasting subject can be developed by, say, recalling a particularly brilliant game with someone who has had sufficient interest to have watched it.

My message in this simple chapter is this. Like all the best things in life, it requires thought, much thought and more and more thought, before you become a worthwhile conversationalist and are regarded as 'good company'.

2

THE GOOD CONVERSATIONALIST

Most people who wish to be good conversationalists have a clear mental picture of the kind of person they would like to be.

There he is, over among that crowd of people – this person we would like to be. He is the most important individual in the group, not because he is socially the most prominent, nor the most influential in business, nor the wealthiest, nor the most handsome in the gathering.

He is its most important member because without him conversation would end and the group would disperse.

He is vital because he is holding a number of people together in such a way that individuals are chatting happily to their neighbours. Were he to withdraw, the company would separate into knots of two or three people; there would be no general theme and some of them would begin to feel lost or bored.

It is profitable to study this man closely, to see what kind of man he is, no less than to observe exactly what he is doing and how he is doing it.

This examination is the purpose of our book. It is written in the conviction that most of us *can* succeed in conversation. Study of conversation, together with experience in drawing people out in fluency of both thought and speech – and that is the foundation on which the art of conversation rests – shows that success in conversation does not belong just to people who have some facility of speech (amounting sometimes to glibness) joined to a superficial amiability. Much more surely it belongs to those who study the nature of conversation, see for themselves the principles underlying it and make themselves expert in the methods by which true conversation is promoted.

None of these requirements, neither the study nor the understanding nor the practice of the means of conversation, is beyond anyone's grasp.

With this in mind (and you may put a question mark after it for the moment, if you are doubtful about it) and before going on to consider this expert conversationalist who is our ideal – let us pause to note the differences between the ready talker and the man who can make conversation.

This book does not aim to help everyone acquire only a smooth flow of words plus an assumed agreeableness of manner. Such verbal fluency with insincere geniality must be discarded by all who would make themselves proficient in the art of conversation. As you will see more clearly within a few pages, some of our best conversationalists were not always pleasant to their companions and, oddly enough, often spoke little.

IMPORTANCE OF LISTENING

Whereas one might assume a book on conversation sets out only to make you a good talker, it must, to achieve its purpose, also ensure you become a good listener. Whether speaking or listening is, on balance, the more important in conversation you will decide for yourself in due course. You will at least have no doubt that the silences of a conversationalist are as necessary to him as is his ability to express himself clearly and interestingly.

Examine again the man whom we mentioned earlier, who was the centre of a lively conversation.

It will quickly become obvious that he is holding his group of friends together by keeping a firm grip on *their* interest. The men and women around him are not necessarily especially interested in him. At times they may even appear to have forgotten him. They are interested in what they are discussing.

From time to time he says something which draws attention to himself or he tells an anecdote which makes the others laugh or which re-launches the conversation with fresh vigour and possibly in a new direction. Perhaps five or even ten minutes pass sometimes without his speaking again.

What, then, is he doing? Why? We shall spend much of this book in answering that.

Here, we are content to notice his activities. Occasionally, for instance, he may reply to something said to him – when he does so what he says is usually amusing or witty and frequently brief.

If he tells a story, we notice that he does not do so for the sake of the story. That is to say, his stories are not only told for the purpose of entertainment. They always help forward the conversation, providing a new viewpoint, offering fresh evidence one way or another or perhaps changing the direction of the conversation. They smooth the way to further exchanges of ideas.

Now he is expressing his own point of view about the subject being discussed. Next he turns to a companion to invite another opinion. Later, he may quote something he has heard or read. All the time, we observe, he is concentrating on one thing . . . the interest of those around him. Seemingly without effort he is keeping that group of men and women interested, both in each other and in the topics of conversation which succeed each other without pause. These people are making conversation among themselves and enjoying it. It is his aim they should do so.

The secret is that he knows how to discover what these people like to talk about and how to ensure that they develop their subjects along lines of wide general interest. Because he knows those two things people say he is 'good company'. Without necessarily knowing why they like to be with him, to talk to each other when he is present. They are aware that he always makes conversation easy and pleasant.

Now that we have noticed so much, we begin to understand why he is always successful in talking to people, whether socially among acquaintances or more intimately with his friends. His interest is in conversation as well as in people. In these two interests he is never insincere, never merely a chatterbox. Only the trained observer may notice how little he says but how suitable that little is for promoting fluency of conversation among those in whose company he happens to be. His gift is to pull people out of their shells.

We now come to our second main point. You may be inclined to feel at this stage – 'Well, I think that I realized all these facts before. My personal difficulty lies not so much in wondering what a good conversationalist is and what he does as in trying to discover how he does it. To some extent I know what is wanted but I do not know how to supply it myself.'

This is the start of our inquiry into the art of making conversation and friends. From here we can progress step by step through the principles and methods which produce that conversational ease which is the hallmark of the expert.

BEGIN BY THINKING ABOUT INTEREST

You can prove that this is the most fundamental part of a conversation by trying the experiment of talking to a boy of twelve. There is only one way of making certain that he will talk back – that he will actually exchange ideas with you instead of merely giving monosyllabic answers to your questions. Talk to him about his stamp album or his bicycle – his pets or favourite sports. If you are not wise enough to base the conversation on something which interests him he will soon lapse into an unhappy silence.

This applies equally when talking with adults – *you must make interest the foundation of your exchange of ideas.* Now and again you may find that the other person is not interested in any of the things you mention. Not every woman wants to think or talk about the furniture in her home or her children; not every man is a keen gardener or football fan. Here as always the exception proves the rule, but it should not be too difficult to find out what other interests a person has and conversation will readily follow your discovering the lines along which the particular mind runs most easily.

If you once grasp the fact that conversation rests on interest, whether personal or social or professional, and that without interest there can be no sustained conversation, you accept the most important truth as to why and how people talk to each other.

Here is what one of the friends of that supremely good conversationalist, Dr. Samuel Johnson, wrote about him. 'He encouraged others to speak, especially young men, and paid due attention to what they said.'

This is an illuminating statement because it leads to another point we shall shortly make and because it corrects a misunderstanding about Johnson. He is believed by many to have been an incessant talker who expected others to listen to him while he discoursed on any subject. This is untrue. Johnson was capable of sustained speech as are all good conversationalists – and in such a way that his listeners wanted to continue listening. He was a great and fascinating talker. But talking and conversation are different things – and what made Johnson outstanding was his excellence as a conversationalist.

'*He encouraged others to speak.*' In other words he found out the things in which they were interested and helped them to talk about those things. Reading Boswell's famous *Life* will bear that out.

'*Especially young men.*' Johnson was rightly reputed to be one of the most learned thinkers of his time. He was the kind of man in whose presence anyone might easily be silent and self-conscious. Yet we are assured that he was so anxious for other people to do the talking, and to tell him *their* ideas, that he took special care to encourage young men to converse with him. That is, people who above all others might be expected to be diffident in his company. Young men, too, are inexperienced. They are usually not the best read nor the best informed people. If they are sensible, they realize that they are unable to meet older people equally in an exchange of mature and informed opinion. All too often they may have experienced among their seniors, usually not endowed with Johnson's knowledge or depth of thought, that irritable intolerance 'Don't talk nonsense!' which keeps so many people silent.

Whenever people spoke to Johnson he '*paid due attention to what they said*'.

He was determined to learn the interests of other people and enable them to speak of those things.

The important lesson here for the aspiring successful conversationalist is that conversation is not a means by which you can empty your mind of all that is in it but an art by which to promote an exchange of ideas which is useful to all who are talking with you.

Note well one implication in what we have discovered about Johnson – *he appreciated the best qualities of those in his company.*

Keep this in mind. Not every quality in the minds or characters of our friends or acquaintances can claim our admiration and when the traits which displease us are apparent it may be difficult to conceal our reactions and not express them.

Johnson himself sometimes handled his friends roughly. Many of his remarks to them were ill-mannered, ill-humoured, untimely and not infrequently devastatingly critical. One finds, however, that these exhibitions concern Johnson the man rather than the conversationalist; they were indulged when Johnson was being pestered by importunity or was in the mood for man-to-man argument rather than a genuine exchange of views. Even where we find the doctor meeting new acquaintances uncouthly (and his first meeting with Boswell is the classical example of his humorous boorishness) we notice that he soon sought opportunity to make them feel at their ease with him.

Most of us are at times guilty of impatience and haste. This is not inconsistent with a resolution to discover the best qualities in the people we meet. And this resolution is essential to successful conversation for, while a knowledge of the interests of others is the foundation on which talking with them rests, it is not in itself sufficient to make conversation all that it should be. Without a more human element it will remain artificial and impersonal. We must know and like something in people before we can talk to them with sincere interest. There must be sympathy – which does not necessarily imply agreement.

APPRECIATING OTHERS

I believe that this was in Johnson's mind when, in the course of one of their early meetings, he told Boswell that he liked to engage young men in conversation because, among other reasons. *'they have more generous sentiments in every respect'*. Their views might be ill-formed and immature. Their judgements might be hastily formed. Their statements might be too dogmatic and self-assured. All these defects must have been irritating to Johnson, but they did not make him impatient. In them he saw only the eagerness of youth, zest for life, alertness of mind and a will to join as men in the company of men. Instead of 'I'm old enough to be your father' his unspoken reaction was: 'There is much to be said for being young.'

We must try not only to discover the interests of the people we meet but to appreciate whatever is good about them; even about the things which appear to us to be their faults.

In his intercourse with the great orator, Edmund Burke, Johnson came to the conclusion that Burke preferred talking to listening. Once he complained, *'So desirous is he to talk that if one is speaking at this end of the table he'll speak to somebody at the other end.'* Annoying though this must have been, he did not let it prevent his seeing the qualities which made Burke eminent even in the excellent company to which both men were accustomed. Many times he acclaimed Burke as an excellent man with whom to hold conversation, praising his power of perpetual thought, referring to his great wisdom and pointing out his gift for making any subject interesting to his audience.

Curiously his complaint against Burke appears to have been ill-founded. Often Burke was more anxious to be in Johnson's company than the doctor found convenient. After spending an evening at Johnson's he remarked to a fellow guest 'How great Johnson has been tonight!' The man agreed but expressed his wish that they might have been able to enjoy more of Burke's own talking. 'Oh no.' Burke answered heartily, 'it is enough for me to have rung the bell to him.'

Here we have an outstanding example of two accomplished conversationalists, each eager to help the other to open out his views on matters which interested him and each eager to appreciate the best in the character of the other.

3

THOUGHT DRIFT

After introducing the subject of conversation as an art it would be easy to continue by further consideration of the successful conversationalist. I could consider the qualifications of mind and heart which he enjoys, or some of his methods, such as his use of anecdote or repartee.

These subjects I postpone, however, for later chapters, since there may be readers who by now will say: 'This is all true, no doubt. But it does nothing more than hold before me a picture of what I want to be. The more I look at it, the more sure I am I shall never achieve it.'

Such timidity can be conquered! It stems from an unsound conviction that you are often at a loss 'for something to talk about'. I hope to remove this fear.

Nine people out of ten who are hesitant about their ability in conversation suffer from the fear of failure.

Many of these good people are both ambitious and competitive but they suffer from a needless compulsion to forever compare their own prowess with that of their (arguably) more successful fellows. This useless checking on themselves is what leads to the error of believing it is always *they* who are 'at a loss for something to talk about' and in turn to the self-indulgent misery of thinking what a disgrace they are. These irrational lines of thought *are* depressing, and untrue! Giving them house-room clouds and blocks out the very search for topics so earnestly desired. Not to mention the dejected facial expression that goes with them to boot! It pays to observe instead the many silences *everyone* has – but most folk don't worry over. Self blame is the insidious destructor, feeding on itself. 'Laugh and the world laughs with you . . .'

Admittedly the main difficulty in opening a conversation is in knowing what to talk about. That is inevitable as our first job is to find and hold the other person's interest. If we don't know what interests him, then we don't know what to talk about. Sometimes the difficulty is increased by the diffidence or conversational inexperience of our companion. He cannot frame a reply which will promote conversation. He can neither seize the rope we fling him nor throw one to us to cover the gap between us.

FINDING A TOPIC FOR CONVERSATION – AUTOMATICALLY

Some people even appear to resemble the unhappy man pictured in Dryden's lines:

> 'He trudged along, unknowing what he sought,
> And whistled as went, for want of thought.'
> > (*Cymon and Iphigenia*, line 84.)

I say they appear to resemble this man, for everyone has thoughts, ideas, opinions and wishes. Conversational difficulty arises because these attributes seem to dissolve into nothing when needed. The mind becomes blank, the thoughts frozen – ignorance of technique redoubles consequent fear. Fluency of thought and expression seem ever distant. The methods outlined here are designed specially to enable you to attain both.

Far from finding that you cannot marshal your thoughts easily, you will find that you can think without effort on eight or nine topics of conversation within a minute or two of needing them. You will discover that if as suggested you make the slight initial effort required to start the psychological process your mind will not empty but will automatically *fill up* with ideas.

Notice that word *automatically*. In it lies the secret of fluency of thought. The method explained here works according to nature; it is not artificial but follows the laws governing the mental processes. Consequently as soon as the method is used the mind responds and ideas move about it abundantly. The psychoanalysts have used a similar method, known as 'free-association'. To understand why this is so and to feel assured that what you are reading is solid and helpful, consider for a minute or two how your mind works.

The thought now going into your mind is entering a room already fairly full of ideas, and it fits comfortably among the other thoughts present there. These thoughts are constantly changing. This morning, for instance, you received certain ideas while you were reading your newspaper, from conversations overheard while you travelled in the bus or train, from things which you saw in shop windows, in the office or at home. Most of these ideas have already left your mind. Where did they go?

At the same period during which these thoughts occupied your attention other thoughts came into your mind which certainly did not enter, like those of the first kinds, from the outside world. For example, when the bus back-fired, you thought of a rifle shot and afterwards of war, or of a murder which took place in the film you saw last night. Again, when you noticed a green hat in a shop, you thought quite automatically of a friend who has a similar hat.

These thoughts came from inside you. Where did they come from?

WHERE THOUGHTS ARISE

It is clear that your conscious mind, which is incessantly receiving thoughts both from within and without, has a much larger mind at the back of it, a subconscious mind which is like a room with walls capable of indefinite expansion. Its walls are able to be enlarged almost to an unlimited extent. Into this lumber room the conscious mind pushes every thought, impression or imagination of interest for which the outside world and its activities are responsible.

Here in the store room everything is registered and fitted away. Even during hours of sleep enormous activity goes on in the subconscious mind. *We could call it the store-away mind.*

Realizing this, people sometimes say, 'I will sleep on it.' It is a common experience for them to find on waking that their mind has formed an answer to their problem in the night. The ever active subconscious mind has worked on the problem while they slept.

Recognize that in this store-room we have the experience of all our years to draw upon as topics. Thus we are not limited to the conventional and obvious weather, politics, health, hobbies and gardening. Any of these may provide a good source of conversation, of course, but I want you to grasp control of the wider choice available to you.

CHOICE FROM THE STORE-AWAY MIND

The subconscious mind, without our being fully aware of the process, is always preparing and storing subjects for conversation. Ideas which we have bundled into it have not only been sorted and stored, but fitted together and related. Fact has been linked to fact, thought to thought, by association of ideas, so that a sequence of thought is prepared. Because of this activity, conversation is, at this first stage, only the tapping of an inexhaustible spring. It's wonderful, isn't it! Tap the spring and the resources behind it flow out by their own abundant energy.

Apart from the comparatively slight initial effort needed to open the mind to receiving ideas the rest of the work consists of directing the energetic flow of thought which enters the active or conscious mind. If you wish you may call the method we are studying the tapping of the mind's resources.

To appreciate to the full the possibilities resulting from this simple act, think of the mind as an ocean and not as a spring. Your thoughts might be likened to fishes swimming there. They are of many species. Moreover, they move in shoals. In the same way your ideas are separate and distinct from each other, but they are sorted out and placed close to each other by the subconscious mind.

If you bring one idea to the surface of the mind, it will be followed by others which are drawn up with it by the lines of inter-relation existing between all ideas which can be associated with each other. If we like we may fish with a line or a net, either looking for a certain idea or for a shoal of similar ideas from which to choose precisely what is needed.

Here is the beginning of our method of acquiring thought fluency. That is why this chapter is entitled the 'Thought Drift'.

As a start, let us be content to let the mind do its own drifting while we watch what happens.

The process is no more haphazard than deep sea fishing. To the uninformed observer, drifting appears a casual, happy-go-lucky affair. The man in charge of it, however, knows well that it is wholly purposeful and that nothing is left to chance.

MENTAL 'DRIFTING'

To start your own mental drifting, take a pencil and a sheet of paper. Look at one of the many objects around you at the moment ... the electric light, a chair a vase.

Close your eyes for a moment and do not think.

Simply let your mind drift round one of these objects.

After a moment or two, note on your paper the ideas which came into your mind. It is not necessary to our purpose that you should write them in the order in which they came into your mind.

As we are going through this training together, let me show you what happens to me so that you will know you are doing what is required. I look at a chair; then I allow my thoughts to drift about it. My mind leaves the chair, but does not actually go astray. It thinks of wood. Wood means forests .. peaceful, sunny days when I have holidayed in the pleasant countryside.

Automatically I think of a friend who shared those days with me. In imagination I see her, recall her clothes, her voice ...

Well there, we can break off the line of thought which has, by the mind's own activity, been offered to me. Notice that I made no effort at all except that first slight one of focusing the mind on one object. The thoughts came much more quickly than one could write them down.

THOUGHTS COME QUICKLY

Now we look at these ideas separately. Chair – wood – forests – holidays – a friend – clothes – fashion – sounds. I wonder where it might have ended if it had been allowed to continue. As it is there are seven possible subjects of conversation, excluding the chair with which we started. This is, of course, only the beginning of our method, merely an indication of the way in which you allow your mind to work for you.

A first step in finding 'something to talk about' is to let your mind wander off on its own after you have given it a starting point (and what that point may be is entirely unimportant) so that it works its way naturally forward from something suggested to it by one of your senses. A sight, a sound, a smell, any sense perception is adequate for the beginning of our method.

The second step is to generalize the ideas so produced, if this is helpful. For instance, my friend would not necessarily be interesting to anyone else as a conversational topic, so that idea I could generalize into friendship or friends or goodwill. It could be generalized and developed much further but we don't want to go too far afield at the beginning.

What happens in this second stage is still automatic. Just as your mind will draw out one thought after another for you, in a sequence of ideas, so if stopped at any one of them it will spread all round it. Or, if you prefer the illustration, if stopped from moving in a vertical line of thought at one point, it will then proceed from that point towards all points of the compass. You can choose to follow it along any one of these developing lines of thought. Thus from the mental image of your friend, you might generalize the idea into friendship, and arrive at an idea about international goodwill. You halt at this point because it ties up with an incident in the newspaper which struck you as interesting or significant. Here for example may be your precise subject for conversation.

You may want to rush ahead to see where we go from here. Do that if you wish, but it is better to learn step by step and not to proceed from one step to the next until you have considered and *practised* the point dealt with.

Before going further, and as a reassurance in case you have that 'my mind goes blank' worry, notice how easy and almost entirely effortless this method is. It doesn't mean that at the very beginning of a possible conversation you pass into a kind of starry-eyed trance, during which the other person decides to leave before you become dangerous! What you are reading now, and will shortly practise, actually happens in seconds. It will take less time to go through than you might use to light a cigarette.

This is because it is entirely natural. It is the way in which your mind wants to work. If it is unfamiliar and now sounds strange to you, it is only because this may be the first time you have analysed how conversations actually begin inside you.

CONVERSATION IS NATURAL

It is therefore in marked contrast with the feverish efforts which some people make in order to 'get a conversation going'. The harder they try to find 'something to talk about' the more self-conscious they become, until they understand all the agonies of the goggle-eyed, semi-paralysed characters in whom P. G. Wodehouse so happily specialized. Efforts to 'think of *something*' are blocking the efforts which their minds are making to suggest something.

The secret of starting a conversation is to let your mind do the work for you. It will, always and unfailingly, if you give it the chance to do so. This method, of natural, effortless thinking is the opportunity it needs.

Now let us look at another thought sequence.

To let my mind begin the sequence I looked at a reading lamp on my desk. Here is the chain of ideas which automatically came to mind within a minute of my noticing the lamp and allowing my mind freedom to wander.

Lamp – Inventions – TV – Actors – History – Time – Purpose of Life – Family – Starvation – Disease – Science – and Goodwill. As a mere list of ideas it is more or less incomprehensible. Notice that this fact is unimportant, since we did not set out to find a sequence of thought but rather a number of conversational subjects. And here they are, all twelve of them.

How did the mind find them for itself. The *Lamp* recalled to me the *Invention* of the electric bulb, and I remembered an excellent science programme I once saw about the life of Edison. This brought to my mind certain screen *Actors* and with this recollection came to mind (I can't see the connection yet, but this is irrelevant to our purpose) a character part played by Dustin Hoffman in a film about Watergate.

Since *History* is one of my reading hobbies, the remembering of this film inevitably led my mind to history and so to the idea of the passage of time. Instantly I thought of the years that had gone and that were to come and my mind considered the *Purpose of Life*. This in most men's hearts is perhaps the creation and bringing up of a *Family*.

In war the first care of men and women is for the children, an idea which hardened into the more definite thought of the *Starvation* suffered by children in wars. Hunger leads to *Disease*, so that medical *Science* is called on for help. There is no danger that by using the method explained here your mind will become standardized or made to work according to a pattern. Every mind uses the method in its own way and with results different from those reached by others.

The purpose of this process is not to find a line of thought but a number of items. To try to use this line as the backbone of a conversation would be fatal to the interest of anyone with whom you might try to talk. For one thing, several items in it are probably dull except to the mind which thought of them. Even to this mind they were attractive only because they occurred in certain associations of ideas.

No, our aim is not to inflict all these topics on someone nor to drag him through the whole line of thought which my mind only and on only this occasion joined together. *We have merely shown how to discover a number of conversational topics by the aid of which we may discover where another person's interests lie.* Once this has been found conversation becomes possible.

For the moment we may be content to know that we have a method by which, after a slight initial effort, the mind automatically provides us with a variety of possible subjects. With the help of Thought Drift we now have them present in the conscious mind. Aware of them and of the person to whom we are going to talk, we can select one topic which seems most likely to arouse his interest. If there is no useful response, we can fall back on another subject from our list.

How does all this work out in practice?

At this stage we possess only an outline of conversational possibilities. This outline is in its most awkward form being only a succession of knots on an invisible thread. The timid talker may, for instance, imagine himself with a mind charged with frighteningly unrelated ideas which he is to cast one after another at some casual acquaintance. The results would be disastrous.

However, such horrors are nearly always averted naturally. For while we try one topic or another in conversation, our companion's mind is also drifting to some purpose. Our mention of a subject starts *him* thinking. What you say causes some reactions in his mind, any of which may serve to make this first beginning a good opening for an exchange of ideas.

OPENING A CONVERSATION

It is important to appreciate that when you introduce a topic of conversation you are not expected to deliver the whole of it as it is in your own mind. Conversation is easier than making speeches . . . *far easier*.

The shy person is apt to forget that he is speaking to another mind which normally responds to suggested ideas. It is usually this response, rather than your first proposal, which is the beginning of conversation. To illustrate, if I mention rheumatic twinges and have in mind a remedy which I consider useful, my friend may make such a reply that my cure need never be mentioned. He may react by referring to his own treatment or by introducing some further topic of medical discovery, or he may even declare his emphatic conviction that rheumatism is largely a product of incorrect eating!

For the purpose of conversation it is unimportant what opinion he advances. What matters is that his interest has been aroused; the conversation launched. Your partner has revealed something of his own mind. *You are no longer dependent on your ideas* but can make use of those which your companion puts forward.

The following might help you get some practice.

EXERCISE

1. Starting from some object perceived by your senses (a table, the perfume of flowers, music, the weight or smoothness of something you are handling, the flavour of a cigarette) – let your thoughts drift without any attempt to guide them. Make a mental note of each idea which occurs to you.

2. If any item in your list is particular, such as a *garden*, make it general, i.e. *gardening* or *gardens*. This widens the scope, making it more suitable for conversation.

3. Use this method in talking to a close friend with whom you feel at ease. If the first topic or two which you select from the list provided by your Thought Drift does not cause the desired response, you will thus not be specially upset and will find it easier to persist in proposing further subjects to discuss.

4

GIVING IT DEPTH

A superficial conversation passing lightly over a variety of topics without pausing long on any one of them is difficult to sustain.

The purpose of this chapter is to explain how thinness in conversation may be avoided. Even the lightest talking requires some depth of thought in order that it may interest.

Some suggested topic may not secure the interest we hoped. Suppose for example that a person has responded to the general subject of *plants*. This alone may be adequate to maintain a hold for a few minutes, but unless the subject is given depth the conversation resting on it must necessarily remain vague in its details. Probably this happens because, although the topic caught the other person's interest, it failed to secure that *kind* of interest in which he, perhaps, specialized. Too often a conversation ends abruptly only because its topic was presented head-on, so to speak. Try to raise subjects in such a way that they can be widened to enable people to speak about that part of the subject which interests them.

In order to talk about anything a man must make an effort – he must make known where his interest lies in the subject you have introduced in a general way. It is from this effort that the inexperienced or timid person shrinks. He is unwilling to make known what the subject means to him, possibly out of lack of confidence in his own opinion or because he assumes you to be more knowledgeable. Without the initial effort the conversation dies. Always play your part.

There are some subjects, for instance, *gardening*, about which people talk readily. It may be the expert guiding the novice, or two enthusiasts discussing sweet-peas but such subjects are good because usually nobody is at all inhibited about them.

Apart from these few subjects, the conversationalist must make two moves before he can be reasonably sure of success. The first is to have ready a series of possible topics and we have considered the method of preparing them. The next move is to propose aspects of whichever of these topics appear to interest your audience. Success requires experience and I shall try to outline a method which you can practise.

When you detect a response to the general topic you have introduced – while your friend or friends are discussing it in the usual conventional way – *your mind* should be dividing the topic into its categories.

This may sound formidable. It is, in fact, so simple that you can train yourself to do it automatically. A trained mind is so alert that the mention of a subject sets it off discovering a number of aspects within seconds.

Reflect on the topic already mentioned, *Plants*. As a conversational opening it has many possibilities but they may be lost unless we can instantly find where other people's interests rest. Are our companions interested in hot-house or open-air plants? Winter, Spring, Summer or Autumn growing? Or perennials? The cultivation of flowers for the table or of herbs? It will be a waste of time to discuss your ambition to grow the perfect rose if your friend is only interested in the destruction of fruit tree pests. But if you know another friend who is expert with fruit trees you might make a friendly offer to effect an introduction another day. Good groundwork for cultivating friends!

Develop the habit of classifying general topics. In this way you can discover which department or aspect is likely to be of use in any particular conversation.

To acquaint yourself with this you might practise the following exercise.

EXERCISE

With pencil and paper – write the word 'Trees' at top centre. Now think. The subject is capable of divisions and sub-divisions as well as introducing a number of associated ideas. You may find your mind hurrying from one activity to another, dividing trees into hardwoods, conifers, and so on, while at the same time thinking of Christmas trees or of the tree on which Judas hanged himself, perhaps not all of them as quickly as that. Yet in some instances, possibly, more ideas than those will arrive in that space of time. Continue thinking for a minute or two longer about the general subject, *Trees*. Jot down the ideas which occur to you until you have about a dozen.

Look at your notes. Sort out and classify the ideas. Note and it is important to do so, that this is the stage at which you classify. *To do so sooner would disperse the flow of ideas*.

Later, you should find that you can separate ideas into categories or link them according to their affinities as they come to you. Unless you have experience in allowing your mind to pick up ideas, it is likely to be best to wait before classifying.

When you have allocated your ideas you may find something like this:

TREES

Trees in national symbolism (English Oak, Canadian Maple).

Famous old trees (the vine in Hampton Court).

Famous giant trees (such as the Californian redwoods).

Sayings connected with trees (Up a gum tree; You shall know a tree by its fruit).

The uses of different species of trees (from masts to pit-props and matches).

Popular beliefs about trees (the treacherous elm, etc.).

Nature's uses of trees (preventing soil erosion, etc.).

In making this list I have been playing the game with you. I have not spent more than a minute in letting the general subject drift in my mind but have followed the rules as much as possible. I relaxed and allowed my mind to wander.

ANOTHER EXERCISE

This time with a slightly different slant which takes us nearer the heart of the matter.

Take the word 'Communications'. Do not try to think quickly but allow your mind to freely associate with the word, considering it from all sides. Your purpose is to perceive the divisions into which the subject may be analysed.

When you believe you have compiled a reasonably complete list, mark it on your sheet of paper methodically. In the following summary of divisions, notice how each division is subdivided. The analysis could have gone further, of course, but for the purpose of providing conversational topics it does not need to do so.

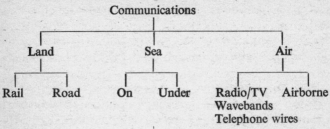

From here the mind advances quickly to divide under-sea communications into, for instance, marine cable and submarine transport. The idea 'airborne' brings to mind airmail, or air passengers or air transport of goods. There are also different kinds of aircraft; rocket, helicopter, Concorde ... A conversation might 'take wings' with such a flow of subjects and lead away from 'Communication' to supersonic speeds, physical science, peace, religion, and so on.

Our examples show how the method of deepening a general topic can assist a conversation to pass rapidly from its opening subject to others only remotely allied to it.

Remember, in talking to others, we do not try to conduct them only along our own line of thought or force them to every apparent division of a subject. Our purpose is to discover a number of possible general topics and to deepen such of these as are of interest to our companions. They too will be advancing stimulating ideas for discussion so there's no need to monopolize!

CHANGE AS YOU GO

Should your first choice of subject bring a poor response move on to another; if interest is shown, deepen the topic by mentioning one or more of its divisions. In the same way subdivide any division to which your companions react favourably.

This is but a stark theoretical outline – in practice it all becomes easier. Conversation is an exchange of ideas between two or more people. All the work is not left to one even though it may be that only one will know how to make good conversation possible. When he has succeeded in engaging the attention of another the latter begins to contribute his share. The responsibility is shared. The opener's part changes. From being the soloist, he passes into the trio or quartet for the time being. He can be content to join in the talking, or, whenever he considers it wiser, allow the conversation to proceed without him, mindful of La Bruyere's observation: 'Conversation consists much less in showing a great deal of it than in causing others to discover it.'

We all have memories of incidents which are interesting to other people. Let us use them in conversation. The result is increased interest and the conversation is both sustained and freshened because a personal angle has developed in it. It is like stepping off a high-road into an unexpected byway.

If you are aware of this small but important piece of technique you can gain pleasure and profit by watching it in use, apart from your own employment of it. Since it is natural, most people use it occasionally but without necessarily realizing what they are doing. It is as natural to conversation as breathing is to the speaker and for this reason is all the easier to use simply and without being artificial.

In summary, what we have studied about the Thought Drift and how to develop it may be expressed in three words, Discover, Divide, and Spread. First find your topic, by having a series of subjects ready for use and introducing them until one of them strikes the spark of interest. Then divide the subject into its natural parts and spread the possibilities, occasionally at least, by introducing personal associations of ideas connected with the topic which has been established.

The following exercises, which introduce some minor means of development not found in the previous text, may be useful for practice.

EXERCISES

1. (*a*) List the topics derived from a Thought Drift starting from one of the following: a cat; a beetroot; a statue; a musical chord; the colour red; a salad bowl; a horse; not being able to think of anything to say.

   (*b*) Develop any topic obtained in this way dividing it into such parts as it seems to fall into naturally.

2. (*a*) Take any other topic from your list and connect some personal association with it, either to reveal it as it is in your own mind or to provide an opportunity for the conversation to pass from that topic to another.

   (*b*) Do you know any anecdote which will illustrate any of the points which came into your mind while you were practising (*a*) as above? How would you relate the story?

3. Suppose that someone has tried to open a conversation with you by mentioning one of the following topics – Dentists – Games – News Bulletins – Hobbies – Reading – Cost of Living – Spring – Changing Your Mind. This is not an inspiring list, but gives you an excellent opportunity to practise making the conversation fresh and original. Let your mind drift round the topic you have selected and decide which is the most promising idea which occurs to you.

4. Take the topic, in the above list, which you like least and deal with it as in 2 (*a*).

5

BACKGROUND TO CONVERSATION

I have endeavoured to answer the first of the two questions which arose at the beginning of the book – What shall I talk about? Now I consider the answer to the further question – how shall I talk?

This involves the technique of continuing conversation with pleasure and interest when it has been established. Let us examine the main ornaments and personal qualities which elevate talking from a bare and dry exchange of ideas to a full communication of thought.

We shall study how to talk naturally and convey the contents of our minds easily. We can draw upon all that has been stored by intelligence, memory, imagination, experience and sense of humour, and project ourselves and our thinking, to those among whom we talk. The art of concise self-expression demands an understanding not only of the subject matter but of methods of presenting it.

The development of conversation can be regarded in two distinct steps. In literature, by way of comparison, step one consists of deciding upon those activities which the author knows he wishes to communicate. Step two in writing is the choosing of the form and the style to be used to get across to his readers exactly what he wants to put into their minds. In so far as he is able to choose the correct form, and to use that form successfully, the author is practical in his art. This is true whether he writes serious prose, fiction, allegory based on recognizable fact, verse or any other form. He must choose the right medium and the right technique for employing it, and enjoying it! If he chooses to express himself in verse, he must know what verse demands of him and be able to supply the demand.

The art of conversation is less complicated but it has its own methods, which are chiefly psychological. We must know, in the practical side of this art, just how to say any given thing to a given person.

In approaching our task we should not regard the qualifications of the conversationalist as so many artificial acquirements which we attach to ourselves. They are not like pins in a pin-cushion. By constant practice the technique of good conversation must become part of us. An easy and natural employment of it will never be attained as long as we regard it as an instrument, something outside ourselves. Everything to do with conversation must be regarded as part of ourselves, completely identified with us. The points we are going to consider should form within us what we may call the 'conversational personality'. So natural can the art of conversation become, spontaneous and individual in each of us, that the poet Cowper, who rejoiced in it, could write:

> 'Conversation in its better part
> May be esteemed a gift, and not an art.'
>
> (*Conversation* 1, 3)

As a beginning, we may take up a point referred to in Chapter 2, and remind ourselves that the conversationalist should:

ALWAYS BE A GOOD LISTENER

This may not be appreciated by those who ride roughshod through company, presuming that others *should* listen to their endless monologues. Such people are talkers and not conversationalists. The good conversationalist must learn when to speak and when to be silent.

Think again of the man whom we watched in Chapter 2 – the ideal conversationalist who controlled a discussion both by his silences and his timely interventions. He is no creature of the imagination for his counterpart is to be found among the great conversationalists of whom we have record.

An understanding of what he is doing shows us that the art of listening must be acquired and be sincere and not merely assumed. To listen is an instinct which we must develop. Unless it becomes an acquired habit it will quickly forsake us so that we do not possess a trained ability in conversation.

Good listening does not mean prolonged silence. To say nothing, to contribute nothing to what is said, is of little benefit to you or others. The silence of good listening, however, is attentive. It is a sympathetic silence, in the sense that it offers, in the true meaning of the word, the sympathy of your attention *even when you disagree*. You will soon perceive that you cannot extend this sympathetic listening to anyone without his coming to realize that you *are* anxious to hear him. Your attitude as a conversationalist will become apparent to him, without your saying or doing anything to reveal it, by a dozen details of your appearance and behaviour of which you may be unaware. How you look at him, the inclination of your head, the expressions which flit across your face, the unpremeditated movements of your hands, all convey close attention.

The impression he receives encourages him to express himself (even though he may know you disagree with his views). In this way you are helping the conversation.

The graces of conversation, the qualities which make it thrilling and delightful, require that you make this attentiveness a part of yourself.

GENUINE LISTENING VITAL

Genuinely attentive listening tells your companion that you consider he is worth your regard. It gives him confidence to continue with what he wishes to say. He takes special care to express himself as clearly as he can; he does not hesitate to correct himself; he feels encouraged to venture on an anecdote or comparison which will help his meaning. Your listening is promoting conversation more successfully than any series of comments or interruptions could do.

We have all at some time been compelled to talk to people who interrupted us by a series of interjections, remarks, questions or statements. Sometimes what was said contributed to the subject but often the addition was merely useless. It snapped our thought line, deflected us from our purpose and destroyed the pattern of our words. This illustrates the damage inexperienced or unkind listening can do.

Consider the personal advantages which the habit of sympathetic listening brings to our conversation.

It covers our weaknesses.

None have the ability to talk at large and on many occasions through the day without the risk of falling into faults which will spoil good conversation. If we do more talking than listening, we are likely to make mistakes in what we say or how we say it. We may easily become excited or confused. We may repeat ourselves or tell our anecdotes again in different conversations with the same person. The substance of our remarks will inevitably grow thinner and our jokes become familiar. We may become known as trying people to talk to or perhaps bores.

The discretion of silence saves us from these faults, which are as quickly noticed by others as they are harmful to us.

While we are not talking we can think. We have the opportunity to consider what others are saying and to prepare our replies. *We can also make sure of the reasonableness of what we intend to say*, revise our method of expressing it *and watch for the right moment to do so*. It is good advice to 'think twice before you speak once'.

During periods of listening companions can be weighed up. You can come to know more of their interests so that when your turn comes to speak you can select appealing subjects.

While we listen, we watch. We note changes of expression. We gain an insight into the workings of other minds. We study traits of character as they reveal themselves. We think about what we see as well as of what is said.

The more accurately we observe others the easier it is for us to maintain conversation with them.

The knowledge thus acquired gives us an unobtrusive mastery over the conversation. We can lead it wherever we may wish among the interests of those about us.

The great conversationalists of history used this discipline of silence and attentive listening to gain ascendancy. The minds they addressed themselves to were as familiar to them as favourite volumes in their own libraries. Much practice also gave them the ability to penetrate and readily understand new acquaintances, so that presently their ability to succeed in any company was assured.

We may pass to another advantage of listening. Good listening adds emphasis to what *we* say. A mountain above a valley is more impressive than one rising from a plain. The occasional remark is often more effective than a continuing flow of talk.

This is not because what you say is an interruption nor because people feel obliged to listen to someone who has not taken a very active part. Rather it is because what you say is well thought out in advance.

Your interval of silence has, for instance, allowed you to recall the apt quotation which will illustrate your view better than you could in your own words.

YOU CAN QUOTE OTHERS

Perhaps you can now quote statistics or some authority in your support; it may be that you have recalled a story which will draw attention to the point you wish to make or enable your companions thus to see it from a clearly defined angle. The discipline of silence has kept you collected and resourceful so that what you say is the more welcome, because it is suitably expressed. *The easiest and best conversation is when a man has something to say.*

The emphasis which periods of silence give to your conversation is also due to the fact that you have been able to observe the effect which the conversation is having on those taking part in it. You realize, let us assume, that someone must be interrupted and another person drawn in. You notice, too, the trend of the conversation and have time to consider whether it should be given a new direction or a fresh impulse to sustain it along its settled course. And this should be carefully noted, for too few people are aware of the shape and direction of a conversation. It moves along from idea to idea, losing itself, twisting back upon itself, splitting into various points not clearly noted as distinct from each other, if no one takes the trouble to keep it in hand. This happens because too many are talking and too few listening.

The silences of intelligent conversation are of great value to those who wish to be at their best in any verbal exchange of ideas. For them there is not that danger of which Montesquieu warned when he complained that he often lost an idea before he could think of words with which to clothe it. Instead of being so exposed to mental isolation, they, by timely silences, are fluent in words and ready in thought, for they think both their own thoughts and consider what is being said all the time. They are thus at the heart of the discussion and know well what Hazlitt meant when he commented, 'The soul of conversation is sympathy.'

He once described a friend who was adept at conversation. 'If he repeats an old remark or story, it is with the same freshness and point as for the first time. It always arises out of the occasion, and has the stamp of originality. There is no parroting of himself ... His manner is quite picturesque. There is an excess of character and *naïveté* that never tires. His thoughts bubble and sparkle ... The fund of anecdote, the collection of curious particulars, is enough to set up any common retailer of jests that dines out every day; these are not strung together like a row of galley-slaves, but are always introduced to illustrate some argument or bring out some fine distinction of character.'

Now we must leave sympathetic listening, to consider another principle which must be observed during conversation.

TRY TO AVOID TELLING A MAN HE IS WRONG

You may feel this is a foolish rule for to keep it would make conversation artificial. Yet the rule is an ancient one for all who speak in public, whether before a large audience or privately with friends and life is always the happier and more successful because of it. This will be better appreciated when we understand what it implies.

(*a*) If a man is at fault in a statement or an opinion and you must tell him so, set about the task in a way which will allow him to think or feel that the correction comes, at least in part, from himself. In real life conversation does not always flow with the academic smoothness of a discussion between Socrates and his friends. *People have feelings as well as thoughts,* and even though they wish to be reasonable they may still give way to unreason in their statements, solely because their feelings have been roused. Remembering that the aim of the conversationalist is to promote a continuing exchange of ideas, one would not say, 'Rubbish! Utter nonsense!' in reply to a carefully stated expression of opinion. To do so would be to annoy, and the irritation would not be unreasonable. It would prompt the speaker to a hasty retort, possibly to a passionate or obstinate assertion of a view which he may himself even begin to see is not entirely accurate.

Even if the incident is hurried over, a damaging blow has been struck at the conversation in progress. How much wiser it is to instil the correction or disagreement gently! A slowing up of speech, a delaying of the *tempo* of the conversation, may also be valuable, so as to give the other man a chance to listen carefully to the way in which you differ from him. Try to make your own viewpoint fasten on to something he has said with which you agree; take a principle mutually accepted and reason from that to your own suggestions; take one of your friend's statements and show that it logically leads to your own idea rather than his. These are ways in which you can help your companion to change his view without having to say outright, 'I was entirely wrong.' Face-saving, if you like, but usually the best way.

(*b*) If this cannot be achieved, at least leave him some way of escape. We have all at times had to admit that we made a mistake in what we said, were in error as to fact, or were unreasonable. And most of us know what an unpleasant experience it is, when faced with someone without tact or human understanding to have to climb down every rung of the ladder. Most of us can manage to climb down if we have to in honesty, but we don't care to be made to break our necks in doing so. Rather than do that, we may easily yield to the temptation to resist admitting that we were wrong. Profiting by this experience we may learn to make it as easy as possible for the other man to change his ideas without appearing to have been entirely wrong.

If you are still unconvinced of the value of this rule, which no writer of any authority has ever challenged, take it on faith for a time and practise it. You will discover its usefulness.

A hallmark of men of reason and humility is speedy agreement when they *are* wrong. If you are 'cornered' and see your error it will strengthen your character (and your standing with others) to have the grace to openly admit it, as soon as possible. Even if it is an hour, or some days, later, the wind of anger will be removed from the other person's sails. The goodwill necessary to profitable conversation is re-established. A grudging or partial admission of error however merely causes obstacles which should never arise in the communication of ideas and opinions.

At this stage we may observe another rule, since we are already on the fringes of disagreement in conversation. We need to be sure what our attitude to argument ought to be. An argument is often a healthy and enjoyable activity especially where it is sweetened by wit and anecdote. But generally it is to be avoided in conversation. Admitting that there are exceptional occasions, we must nevertheless make it a rule that we:

TRY NOT TO ARGUE

Experience is worth pages of instruction and in this matter any thoughtful observation of what happens to conversation when argument takes possession will make it unnecessary for us to prove the value of the rule.

You will have noticed how passion rises, conviction is hurled against conviction, exasperation grows and spreads through most of the company while dangerous sarcasm may be introduced. There is a time and place for argument, but it is not in conversation, which it ruins. The following points are suggested.

(*a*) Try to see the other man's point of view. Try to understand his reasons for holding it. As far as may be possible to you, look at it in his way, through his mind, and thus you will understand the view better in itself. And you will be helped when your turn comes to put a different opinion before him. If you can see his view as he sees it, you have a better chance of securing his genuine attention to your criticism of it. Your friend should be assured that you have tried to understand him and you should find that he will make an equal effort to give sympathetic attention to what you say.

(*b*) Tell him what you accept from his statements, what you admire in his opinions or his marshalling of facts. For instance, you may comment on the good sense and logic by which he has arrived at his conclusion, pointing out that your disagreement is with the principle or fact from which he started his line of thought.

(*c*) Be endlessly patient. Keep your emotions and impulses firmly under control. In saying this, I am not one of those who believe that it takes two to make a quarrel; some people are so argumentative and awkward, especially if they are opinionated or inclined to mental snobbery, that it is almost impossible to avoid argument with them. At the same time we know that an argument, which has any other possible end except perhaps a rather unsatisfactory agreement to differ, is useless to conversation. You may need endless patience, and the firmer you are in your own view the more patience you must possess.

(*d*) Always admit your mistakes readily. It is surely needless to write much about this point, especially in view of what has already been considered. We may repeat, however, that willingness to admit any error as soon as you see it goes a long way towards establishing the goodwill necessary to profitable conversation.

On occasions you will find yourself talking to people who are far from argumentative – the diffident, hesitant people who, even when they wish to join in conversation, hold back from doing so. In their company one should remember our next rule, which is that one should:

BE LIVELY, AND EVEN CHALLENGING

This means principally that one should be alert in manner. A smile is more inspiring than much persuasion. A cheerful face is always a good thing to see and too many people have anxious or sad faces without yours being added to the number! A friendly and pleasant approach is more likely to draw people out of themselves than a sober formality.

But do not assume a hearty and forced cheerfulness that is so easily detected for the false thing it is. Anyone who is sensitive shrinks from it, and distrusts those in whom they find it. Instead of this, be as cheerful as you can so as to convey to others a sense of ease and well-being. This is in itself encouraging. Those who know that you can brighten a few minutes will always be glad to listen to you and respond.

If you happen to suffer from shyness in meeting people, remember that your attitude has a discouraging effect on them. You damp down the conversation before it has a chance to start. Sometimes people who feel uncomfortable with new acquaintances incline to hide their fault by blaming others and finding various reasons in them for their own discomfort. These reasons may exist but one should be honest enough to see if the fault is on one's own side. Even if you freeze up and can't think what to say at first, try to show a pleasant aspect to others and not a half-sulky appearance which may be understandable but which is unhelpful and, most of all, is unhelpful to yourself.

On both sides there should be a quiet but cheerful approach. This is less difficult to establish than many suppose.

Finally we come to a rule which is obvious, yet often ignored.

KNOW WHAT YOU ARE TALKING ABOUT

We should be sure of our facts and be modest in our opinions.

I remember listening to a man holding forth about a book which is among our classics but not well known or widely read. It happened that I knew the book and did not agree with his view of it. In the group was a man who I knew to be more able to form a literary judgement than myself, being more widely read and having a sounder literary knowledge. So I held my peace. He did the same.

After the speaker had left us, one of the guests asked this man, 'Why didn't you say something? Did you agree, with everything said?'

'He was too wrong for anyone to discuss the book with him briefly,' was the reply. 'I felt we would have all been bored stiff if one of us had attempted to show him why now; it would have taken so long for him to see the errors of his view. I didn't think it possible for a man to read the book and be so completely mistaken about it.' Then he went on to express a different view of the book, leaving us with an awful sense of X's incompetence. X had even mixed the chapters and incidents, and had introduced one character from a book by a different author.

This illustration is in a sense trivial. But the effect of the incident on X was far from slight, for, if he had afterwards invited our confidence in his judgement in any matter at all, even about his own business which was eminently successful, he would have started at a disadvantage. Each of us had lost confidence in his thoroughness of examination, his powers of analysis, his memory, and his general reliability. A man who can be really inaccurate in one matter is often (though incorrectly) not supposed to be dependable in any.

Inaccuracy as to fact or looseness in thinking can do your conversation harm, if only because it damages the confidence which must exist between people who talk together. *In any conversation, if you feel ill-informed or if you know nothing of the topic being discussed, say so frankly*. That will gain confidence and it will sustain your own confidence. No thinking person distrusts those who admit lack of information, for they can learn; none distrust the man who says he has not thought much about what is proposed, for he shows honesty. You can express theories or say what your guess would be, so long as you make it clear you are doing only that.

These are our rules for successful conversation. In discussing them we have perhaps given the impression that conversation is a sober business. It may have appeared to be a deadly serious exchange of opinions. Such an impression is misleading and we shall proceed at once to examine some of the ornaments which lighten the art of talking well amongst ourselves. An interchange of ideas, however serious it may be, can be whipped up by epigram and quotations, illuminated by anecdote, salted and sharpened by wit.

6

REPARTEE

We turn now to consider some of the garnishes by which conversation is made outwardly attractive, by examining facility in repartee or witty retort. Here, some readers may protest that to analyse anything witty is also to damage it. They may feel that to try and cultivate in anyone the quality of saltiness or droll fancy is almost unnatural and destined to failure. For impromptu, as Molière observed, is the touchstone of wit.

This chapter begins under the handicap of these reflections. I believe, however, that the reader will discover that some practical hints *can* be given. I am not writing about wit itself but confining myself to that part of it called repartee. Repartee is a retort which (in forms which vary but are unexpected and humorous) ingeniously combines or contrasts elements of what has been said. By doing this, the reply checks or closes, advances or opens the topic. For example, here is the answer given to a lady who exclaimed, 'Look at that snowflower braving all this bitter weather! What a plucky little flower!' The reply was, 'Well, there are braver flowers ... think of those which face the English Summer.'

It is not easy to see exactly what that answer does. It is scarcely cynical. Probably its best function is to lighten the conversation, to set gently aside a mild attack of 'gush'. Notice that it takes the statement and, by presenting it from a surprising and original angle, sends it back. In this instance, the reply does it in a form which leaves little opportunity for the speaker to make any further use of the topic; it closes the subject.

As another example there was the agitator who said to the farmer, 'I am determined to get the farm labourer down to an eight-hour day.' The farmer replied, 'Well, for myself, I'd be glad to get an eight-hour night!'

This takes us a step further in our analysis, for it does more than send the topic back to the speaker in a new form . . . in this case, it promotes the conversation by neatly expressing the fact that there is more than one point of view to be considered.

USE OF CONTRAST

You will notice that the method used is that of Contrast. *Night* is opposed to *day*, thereby implicitly contrasting the labourer's long day with the farmer's short night – the hard work of the one but the more prolonged work of the other.

Here then is one source of repartee. By considering the conversation of others and by reviewing your own contributions you can compare what was actually said with what might have been said had contrast been used to enliven and illuminate. In reading, especially good fiction, make a mental note of the methods used wherever you find good repartee. Space prevents the lengthy quotations which would be needed to illustrate this here but that is no loss for it is far more useful for you to find your own examples. In reading P. G. Wodehouse, for example, do not be content to laugh at what is witty but pause to see why it is witty, to notice exactly how the author achieves his effect.

ASSOCIATION OF IDEAS

While contrast of ideas is a common source of repartee, association of ideas is equally fruitful. Here by way of an aside we may slip in some recognition of the fact that Similarity of Sound can give rise to the salted reply, while not degenerating into a pun. For example, I once heard a man cough diplomatically after a remark by a friend of his in a mixed company. His friend glanced at him, half surprised and half amused at the hint, and asked, 'I didn't say anything untoward, did I?' The answer was 'No, I don't think so. But it was getting on towards . . . you know.'

The sound of the question was like a pebble dropped into a pond. It set up ripples of association which spread in the mind of the listener until the sound of *untoward* suggested the form of his answer, that what had been said *was getting on towards what might be considered untoward*.

That point we notice merely in passing, for our chief concern is with Association of Ideas rather than of sounds. Here is a witty reply to an old aphorism that 'The perfect host is one who makes his guests feel at home.' The teasing host replies, 'Yes, even when he wishes they were!' Here the association lies in the words *at home*, calling into mind that place to which we have all at times heartily wished some long tarrying friend, whom we nevertheless wanted to treat with kindliness, would go. The words *at home*, linked with the idea of *perfect host*, showed the speaker that the form of his answer would give effectiveness to his idea and yet, by adding a humorous twist to it, rob it of sourness. Hence the success of the remark.

We come close to bruising the butterfly's wings in examining them but it must be done, for our aim is to see how repartee arises and by so doing increase our use of it. Our

63

studies may also save us from misunderstanding this kind of retort. People sometimes allow themselves to make rude or cutting remarks thinking they are achieving minor brilliance in conversation.

DIVISION OF IDEAS

Next we consider a third method of repartee – division of what is said. A quotation from Oscar Wilde's *The Importance of being Earnest*, gives us an aphorism and repartee.

> 'All women become like their mothers. That is their tragedy.
> No man does. That is his.'

The reply is based not so much on contrast between man and woman as it is founded upon the fact that woman is only half of the race. If someone makes the statement about woman which Wilde wrote in that play, there is an almost instinctive urge to reply by completing the subject, through the addition of man. From here it is only another step to framing the manner of the reply by affirming the opposite of what was said of woman. The thing is, in a sense, the outcome of an automatic habit of mind. In so far as the habit may become almost automatic, it is bad; yet because it does occasionally reveal the right form for a suitable answer, it is useful to practise.

The example given is, however, exceptional because the subject introduced (woman) is seen as one half of the whole (human race). In most repartee arising from Division, the subject is seen as a whole, and the repartee starts because someone divides the subject. Division of this kind is the source of much repartee.

This may be illustrated by the story of two Edinburgh

ministers who took it in turn to preach the Sunday evening addresses. One soaking wet Winter evening, Samuel read prayers and returned to the vestry to find James discarding extremely wet clothing preparatory to donning his surplice. 'I'm wet through to the skin,' James moaned. 'I'll catch my death of cold while I'm preaching!' 'Never fear, James,' remarked Samuel. 'You'll be dry enough when you're in the pulpit.'

This might be mistaken for repartee based on contrast whereas in fact Samuel split the second half of James's remark (about preaching) and applied the result to the first half (about being soaked through). You will find that this formula is frequently discernible in any crossfire of repartee you may read or hear. Another example may be found in a remark I once heard, made by a man who had a reputation for telling lengthy anecdotes. His answer to my interruption showed that he had a ready wit which, to my own pleasure, successfully launched him into his story.

'I'll tell you a story about that. A particularly good one, as it happens.'

'Oh, heavens, not another, old man. Frankly, your stories never seem to have any end.'

'No? Well this one is so exceptionally good that you'll find it hasn't even a beginning!'

Five more possible ways to combat barracking of the kind in which I had indulged can be great fun, as well as renewing your position of master while you tell the story. The first retort runs:

'If *you* keep talking while I am interrupting, you won't be able to hear me think the story out. Now . . . etc., etc.'

The second quick-witted response (in this instance to being told to 'hurry up') goes:

'Oh! O.K., I'll be brief, have you got six hours?'

And the third:

'O.K., I'll come straight to the point and leave out explaining the middle till I wake up!'

The fourth attacks back:

'I'm sorry, I couldn't hear you. Could you go out and then come in again?'

Number five, when someone has called 'come on, get on with it!' runs:

'Steady up Sunshine, I'm just getting psyched up for telling you my story.'

Continuing directly with your story after one of these spots of repartee, leaves the person ribbing you at a loss for words while the humour sinks in; it also retains the attention of the rest of your audience who will have been pleased to see the barracker knocked out by such a rapier thrust. Note the disarming twist in the use of the name Sunshine.

Other examples:

'Why do you ask so many indiscreet questions?'
'But I don't. It's your answers which are indiscreet.'

'My husband is always trying.'
'All husbands are.'

(WILDE – *The Ideal Husband*)

Facility in quick and witty retort may be developed just as every power of the mind may be strengthened and trained. Not only can the mind develop its natural powers of rapid reply but it can learn how to apply these powers so that they may be useful. This may seem incredible or at least unorthodox. To anticipate the objection – that it makes conversation artificial or standardized – it must be admitted

66

that knowledge of the right methods does not always produce the desired results.

Let us further consider the matter by quoting the proverb 'after-wit is everybody's wit'. The proverb recognizes that, reflecting over a previous conversation, one often sees too late the witty answer which could have been given – if it had been thought of in time. This experience may be depressing: for many it is an almost insuperable stumbling block in their progress towards conversational success. Such discouragement is mistaken. This is seen if you realize that what is perceived too late is also perceived early.

That is, what is too late for one conversation is in hand for another. If some appropriate remark is useless for the conversation of an hour ago, it follows that it will be on the tip of your tongue when a similar opportunity occurs.

A very little effort of memory will enable you to have an ever ready store of such repartee to hand.

I hope we have now been able to explode the idea that repartee must be spontaneous *at the moment it is uttered*. In some speakers it appears to be instantaneous but in fact they are simply experienced conversationalists. A similar gift may be developed by others, especially once they realize that most quick replies are merely the surface action of a mind which has thought deeply, worked out replies and trained itself.

Although the listener is rarely aware of it, skill in the use of anecdote, together with what seems to be an inexhaustible fund of stories, frequently derives from practice *plus a handy notebook which is perused before conversation*. There is nothing artificial about this. It is merely adequate preparation. Who would expect a lecturer to speak without the previous ordering of his thoughts and a checking over of his data? Who would expect a vocalist to sing without rehearsal which is, indeed, his constant occupation? And who will be so foolish as to expect success in conversation without a similar and proper preparation? It is worth the effort.

Why not therefore extend your memory bank to include apt repartee? The writing down process itself helps lodge the ideas in your memory.

In case this view has destroyed any illusion, and such an illusion will be even more dissipated presently, pause for a moment to ask yourself whether it makes the least difference to a conversation if the brilliant reply was spontaneous or whether it was part of the speaker's stock-in-trade? Its effect is the same. So why should anyone be disappointed to think that not all repartee is the immediate scintillation of a brilliant mind?

It is understandable to feel, 'How I wish I could sparkle and shine in conversation! How delightful it would be if witty remarks were to rise as rapidly in my mind as bubbles in a brook!'

Such an experience would be delightful. It would also be exceptional to the way the human mind works. If your companion tosses ideas about lightly and amusingly, be assured that he has (probably with tremendous labour) done much thinking and paid attention to the art of expressing himself. His success lies in the fact that he can quickly find and group a variety of ideas, illustrations, anecdotes, quotations and authorities and express them entertainingly. However spontaneous much of his talk may be, its origin is not spontaneous.

There is a passage in Hazlitt's essay 'On the Difference between Writing and Speaking' worth considering.

'The great leading distinction between writing and speaking is, that more time is allowed for the one than the other:

and hence different faculties are required for, and different objects attained by, each. He is properly the best speaker who can collect together the greatest number of apposite ideas at a moment's warning: he is properly the best writer who can give utterance to the greatest quantity of valuable knowledge in the course of his whole life. The chief requisite for the one, then, appears to be a quickness and facility of perception – for the other, patience of soul, and a power increasing with the difficulties it has to master. He cannot be denied to be an expert speaker, a lively companion, who is never at a loss for something to say on every occasion or subject that offers; he, by the same rule, will make a respectable writer who, by dint of study, can find out anything good to say upon one point that has not been touched upon before, or who, by asking for time, can give the most complete and comprehensive view of any question. The one must be done off-hand, at a single blow: the other can only be done by a repetition of blows, by having time to think and do better. In speaking, less is required of you, if you only do it at once, with grace and spirit: in writing, you stipulate for all that you are capable of, but you have the choice of your own time and subject. You do not expect from the manufacturer the same dispatch in executing an order that you do from the shopkeeper or warehouseman. The difference of *quicker* and *slower* however, is not all: that is merely a difference of comparison in doing the same thing ...'

He contemptuously sketches the man whose interest is rather in the exhibition of his own brilliance, as he supposes, than in the studied promotion of good talking together. He has no use for those 'whose chief ambition is to shine by producing an immediate effect.' Such people are represented in his mind by:

'There is F—; meet him where you will in the street, he has his topic ready to discharge in the same breath with the customary form of salutation; he is hand in glove with it; on it goes and off, and he manages it like Wart his caliver ... but, ere you have time to answer him, he is off like a shot, to repeat the same rounded, fluent observations, to others – a perfect master of the sentences, a walking polemic wound up for the day, a smartly bound political pocket book ... What does all this bustle, animation, plausibility, and command of words amount to? A lively flow of animal spirits, a good deal of confidence, a communicative turn, and a tolerably tenacious memory with respect to floating opinions and current phrases. Beyond the routine of the daily newspapers and coffee-house criticism, such persons do not venture to think at all: or if they did, it would be so much the worse for them, for they would only be perplexed in the attempt, and would perform their part in the mechanism of society with so much the less alacrity and easy volubility.'

EXTENDING A CONVERSATION

Let us turn to another type of repartee, which is when one takes what has been said further than the speaker intended or foresaw. This has been called the method of Exaggeration, and the name is satisfactory as long as we do not understand it to imply anything far-fetched. Extend the speaker's line of thought beyond the point to which he has taken it and the result is often illuminating. It also advances the conversation and may introduce a welcome witticism to lighten it.

What is meant may be illustrated by a conversation between Charles II and John Milton, in which the King attempted to rebuke the poet because he had written in support of Charles I's execution. The King suggested to Milton that his blindness might well be a divine punishment for his approval of what had been done by the regicides. Milton replied, 'Sir, it is true that I have lost my eyesight. But if all calamitous providences are to be considered as divine judgements, your Majesty should remember that your father lost his head.'

Notice how this reply keeps (economically) to the two main points of Charles II's attack. It introduces nothing new, but merely extends the King's line of thought.

This method of repartee is excellent because it is allied to a way of thinking which is sound and reliable. Often we are able to see the fault in an argument only if we extend it to its logical conclusion. By carrying an observation to its conclusion, or at least further towards that end, we not only find the answer to it (and it may be one of agreement instead of disagreement) but also the perfect form in which to express it. We arrive at an answer which is logically sound and conversationally admirable.

We return to the question of preparation. Those who study reported conversations may assume that the originals were carefully revised and polished before they were allowed to appear in print. This is true of many *Letters* and even of certain reported conversations appearing in autobiographies. As a rule, however, the fact is that most of the best conversations of which we have record were written down exactly as they were spoken. This may be a disconcerting fact but it is true. Discouragement may well come from it, since it is natural in the knowledge that there are people who can extemporaneously talk with the brilliance of Oscar Wilde, Dr. Johnson, Winston Churchill or G. K. Chesterton to feel that, in comparison with these giants, conversational ability is definitely wanting in us. The quickness of thought, the sharpness of perception, the perfect suitability of wit and reply, the timing of remarks to follow each other so that each shows the perfection of the other, these things, the inquirer properly concludes, are almost superhuman and certainly are not his either to command by intellectual gifts or by study and effort.

This depressing conclusion is based on a mistake or, more accurately, a confusion of thought. It is certainly true that many eminent conversationalists talked as they are reported. Yet it does not follow from this, as we assume it to, that what they said was wholly on the spur of the moment. They spoke immediately but not necessarily by inspiration. What they said was in many instances laboriously prepared.

IMPORTANCE OF TIMING YOUR SHOTS

The right timing of remarks is as important to a conversationalist as it is to a comedian or an actor. From observation you will have decided that one of the differences between a first-class comedian and his inferiors is that his sallies come at the right moments and to strike us just when the new twist of meaning will drive us into an even greater paroxysm of laughter. Perhaps you have experienced the result of bad timing in telling some joke of your own. A remark which you know was extremely funny has fallen flat; perhaps it was introduced when interest in the subject it referred to had flagged, or possibly because it was recounted before the subject had been developed far enough for its full significance to be appreciated. This is a lesson which can be noted in passing.

People who are careful with their conversation not only prepare their remarks before hand but choose the right moment for introducing them. It is interesting to read that

Oscar Wilde was once accompanied, among other mixed company on a ramble, by a lady who was little capable of appreciating his conversational gifts. The rest of the company enjoyed watching him shaping the conversation and leading it towards a climax in which, as their experience of him assured them, one of his glittering aphorisms would be neatly fitted into place. As that climax arrived the lady asked a question not only foolish in itself but wholly irrelevant.

Wilde accepted the defeat meekly and the conversation drifted away on to another topic. What he had in mind to say will never be known. No doubt he found it useful on another occasion but for this time Wilde was forced to leave his *bon mot* unspoken and rather than introduce it at any other than a perfectly suitable place, he was content to leave in apparent waste all his work in building up the conversation.

Similar care has been shown by men distinguished for their powers of repartee, although not in themselves outstandingly witty. Some of its best exponents are men who both think and speak slowly. Their secret lies in the last two words, for these people *speak slowly* in order that they may have time to think. They need time to understand the full import of what is said to them and by dividing and perhaps re-dividing the thoughts of their companions, form their own opinion with its best expression in words.

This process does not detract from the merit of their conversation. Quickness of reply may often win applause because it attracts attention, as anything swift and glittering will do. Yet it is true that speed has little to do with repartee or any part of conversation. No one having any genuine appreciation of the art of talking would suggest that a man's remarks are less interesting or valuable because he makes them a few seconds later than he would have done were he possessed of a quicker mind.

To think and speak quickly need not be among the aims of those who wish to improve their conversation. Speed of thought and speedy selection of effective words will come naturally through practice. They need not be objectives to be secured by special effort. Too often people create for themselves difficulties which should not exist such as the illusion that they cannot become good conversationalists without speed. They imagine they must become rapid talkers which is not so at all.

CONVERSATION IN COLD STORE

Far better than worrying about failure is to start keeping the notebook we have mentioned by the aid of which conversation may be prepared. All manner of uses can be found for such a book; for the moment we will remark only that it can be a useful repository for those specimens of 'after-wit' which become the timely answers of future days. You can record *improved* versions of things you have said or might have said. You can note corrections you may find necessary to statements which you have made.

Finding your own faults is the best way of learning. The entries will be original and will have the benefit of reconsideration as often as you look through the book. Such revision does not in any way deprive the entry of its freshness or spontaneity when it comes to be spoken. On the contrary, these qualities may be acquired because of the revision, with its pruning of a phrase, removal of an unnecessary word or substitution of a sharper, clearer word for one which is blurred in outline. Is this too much work? Not if conversation is your hobby. This notebook is the workshop where the tools of your craft carefully fashion the products of your art.

In addition to filing original comments and ideas you may note the sayings of other people. Some of these will come to you by your reading, listening to the TV or from conversation. Notes of material which is not original provide you with matter for reflection. Without infringement of copyright or permission you cannot quote second-hand but you can compile a mass of worthwhile matter which will mature in your mind until it slowly becomes assimilated and blended in with your own thought. You will find that your mind has thus been enriched by it and even that the verbal forms of your expression have been improved by studying the methods and phrases of others.

This point recurred recently when a man remarked, 'However it may be with others, I like my life to run along comfortable grooves. I feel well settled in them and can go along in my own way.' His companion was of a more adventurous type, since he commented, 'It has always seemed to me that the only difference between a groove and a grave is in depth.'

Was this entirely original? Not really. But it was the spontaneous reaction of one character to another and it expressed itself in a form which the speaker may have acquired from his father, for all fathers have these 'family' sayings, or from a periodical, or from some source which he had completely forgotten. The point about it is that it was almost certainly familiar material produced the more quickly for having been in stock as an idea if not as a phrase.

RESERVES OF THOUGHT
AND CONFIDENCE

In the same way every conversationalist should have a reserve of thought and words which will come to him aptly as required. The building up of reserves is interesting and important. What has matured in the mind until it is a part of you cannot easily be lost. It will not vanish in any excitement or distraction which sometimes accompanies a conversation. It forms the basis of self-confidence. You remain master of your tongue and to that extent of the conversation. It is not a question of inspired thinking or speedy intervention so much as of the assurance which results from a well-stored mind and practice in expression.

7

APHORISM AND EPIGRAM
(apt sayings and verses)

After considering carefully how you may develop ability for repartee let us pass on to the allied subject of aphorisms – pithy and arresting sayings – often inaccurately termed epigrams. In moving on to wise sayings, I should add that the inspiration essential to wit cannot be taught. This might cause pessimism were it not equally true that few people are devoid of some aptitude for witticism and this can be strengthened.

There should be no need therefore ever to feel 'I can never hope to take a part in bright conversation because I cannot say anything suitable myself'.

Consider this definition: 'Tact is the art of refusing a drink without losing it.'

If a companion said that, in the course of conversation, would you appreciate it?

Almost certainly yes! The remark appeals partly because it is true and partly because it is amusingly expressed. You find the same sort of qualities in an advertisement once used for a new razor blade, 'The greatest invention since the face,' and in the statement that, 'Every reform was once a private opinion.'

WIT EXPLAINED AND DEVELOPED

In this pair of aphorisms only one is amusing. Wit is not necessarily amusing but it is 'the knife which sharpens truth to a point'. It is a crisp and clear way of saying something, with such originality as to arrest and commend itself to the memory.

If you have found the quotations so far given attractive, you have within you the qualities of wit which ensure that you can develop your own ability to speak similarly. Set about the task methodically and your latent ability to brighten your conversation by wit in its various forms will become active.

The first step to take is to make yourself familiar with what others have achieved. Read what is recorded of the wit of famous talkers, public speakers, and writers. Later in this chapter a short collection of sayings is given, varying in value as well as in their appeal to different types of mind. Read through it slowly, pausing whenever one of the quotations commends itself to you. Try to discover why it has made an impression on you.

Then see whether you can improve on it, not necessarily by saying exactly the same thing in a different form but perhaps by expressing neatly and arrestingly your own reaction to what you have read. If at first your pencil remains idle, do not be discouraged. The purpose is not the improvement of what is quoted but the beginning of your own effort to speak briefly and originally. It is by practice as well as study that you improve in pithy and clear expression.

All this work can hardly be rushed; it will take time. First you must steep yourself in the sayings of others. A book of quotations makes fascinating reading but you can get along very well without one, by glancing through magazines which add quoted snippets to their pages. Some may provide in one issue enough aphorisms for a week's study. Make the wit of others your familiar atmosphere. Once it has lost its strangeness, once you begin really to feel at home in it, you will find that your own wit will begin to stir.

You will find that you are acquiring the power to express yourself more perfectly, and as a consequence, more strikingly. You will be making the first, possibly rather embarrassing and unsteady steps, towards your goal.

The next step is more experimental but one need not hold back from it, since with many conversationalists it has proved the secret of their reputation for wit.

ADAPTING APHORISMS

It consists in altering words or more or less accepted aphorisms or beliefs. For example, take the definition which says that 'Discretion is the gift which comes to a man when he is too old to need it.'

Many believe the idea but I once knew a quiet young man who did not, at least not always! The saying was a favourite with an elderly man who the chap was, in theory, bound by etiquette to be polite to because of his age and seniority. One day during a luncheon his elderly companion called on him for 'a few words'. It was a wretchedly unfair thing to do, for the youngster was no speaker and he was among men who could all speak off the cuff with ease and humour.

However, the challenge was accepted quietly and the young man spoke for perhaps two minutes – on 'Discretion'. No one had the least doubt whom the remarks were addressed to. 'I am trying to remember,' he said, 'a quotation about discretion which has always seemed to me particularly striking. Although I have heard X quote it many a time, I cannot ... Ah, yes, it is that 'discretion is a gift which ... comes to a man ... when he is too old ... to *use* it.'

If ever a man had his nose twisted in public, this elderly bully experienced humiliation that day. Some years later I came across the unwilling young speaker again. He had transformed his life and was addressing delighted audiences all the year round, earning large fees by doing so.

Here by altering one word the young man could express a totally different meaning. When the opportunity was forced upon him, he not only used it with effect but to the final release of the powers which he, perhaps less than anyone, had suspected to be in him.

I'm not sure who coined the phrase 'The early bird catches the worm' but this aphorism can be neatly turned inside out to give 'The late bird catches the worm which wasn't there for the early bird'. An aphorism here almost changed into an epigram!

While taking care not to be insincere or artificial you will sometimes find a widely accepted 'fact' can be challenged for being mythical. The attempt at exploding the myth helps to draw all the participants into pitching their view into the conversation. The more contentious the challenge the more extended and fascinating the ensuing conversation is likely to be. For example, a frequent, end of conversation, 'stopper' is expressed in the view that an explanation must lie in 'Woman's intuition'. The common idea being that somehow women think differently from men, who therefore cannot hope to understand. Given that women have identical brainmatter to men, it can be successfully argued that *if presented with the same background and facts* of any problem, men and women will easily arrive at the same conclusion. That is if one can assume they have all had the same training in logic. It is not the 'intuition' therefore which arrives at the different answer we may expect from a woman but the differing type of upbringing she is likely to have had.

Occasionally, with a close friend, something he or she always takes for granted, may be challenged with appropriate tact. His or her personal conviction can be put to the test without actually insisting it is a mistaken view. Success here will in the long run be much appreciated providing you tread carefully! You will be respected for standing behind the differing view in which you believe and having the courage to speak up for it. Both conversational rapport and closeness of friendship can be enhanced in this way but beware of being adamant purely for argument's sake. This would soon drive away your friend.

We now come to some famous quotations and some chosen for their interest. They have been grouped under general headings, although some of them could have been classified under more than one of the groups.

PROGRESS. SUCCESS

'When I came to this country, I hadn't a nickel in my pocket. Now I have a nickel in my pocket.'

Groucho Marx.

'Only those who have stopped thinking, or who never started, boast of never having changed their minds.'

Dwight MacDonald.

'Progress is impossible without change, and those who cannot change their minds cannot change anything.'

George Bernard Shaw.

'The man who never alters his opinion is like standing water, and breeds only reptiles of the mind.'

William Blake.

'The three most important bones are the wishbone, the jawbone, and the backbone. The first spurs you on, the second helps you find out, and the third keeps you at it.'
New Zealand Weekly News.

'Assurance is two-thirds of success.'
Gaelic Proverb.

'The only infallible criterion of wisdom to vulgar judgements – success.'
Edmund Burke.

'Progress stops when it ceases to possess individuality.'
John Stuart Mill.

WOMEN

'He who heeds the advice of a woman is a fool; he who heeds it not is lost.'
Spanish Proverb.

'Great-grandmama was adorable; Grandmama was quaint; Mother is old-fashioned.'
Anonymous.

'A little girl said, "I know something I won't talk about." Her father said, "When you grow up, it will be the other way about".'

'Friends – two women angry with the same person.'
English Digest.

'I don't know how you put up with that idle husband of yours.'

'It's like this, mum. I make our living and he makes life worth living.'

'Women read men more truly than men read women.'
Charlotte Brontë.

'Women are born worshippers.'

Thomas Carlyle.

FRIENDSHIP

'When you are down and out, something always turns up –
and it's usually the noses of your friends.' *Orson Welles.*

'It is better to grow a branch than cut off a limb.'
Chinese Proverb.

'It is always better to discuss what is right rather than who
is right.'

Anonymous.

'A man, sir, should keep his friendship in constant repair.'
Samuel Johnson.

ADVERTISEMENTS

'Promise, large promise, is the soul of an advertisement.'
Samuel Johnson.

'Journalism is but the scribbling on the back of adver-
tisements.'

G. K. Chesterton.

BUSINESS, ETC.

'Business? It is a simple matter; it is other people's money.'
Dumas the Younger.

'October is one of the peculiarly dangerous months to speculate in stocks. The next most dangerous months are the other eleven.'

Based on Mark Twain.

'The wise man makes hay of the grass that grows under the other man's feet.'

English Digest.

'When a man is no longer anxious to do better than well, he is done for.'

Benjamin Haydon.

COMPLACENCY

'Let us not be too particular. It is better to have old second-hand diamonds than none at all.'

Mark Twain.

'A great many persons are able to become members of this House without losing their insignificance.'

Beverley Baxter, M.P.

'To love oneself is the beginning of a lifelong romance.'

Oscar Wilde.

'There isn't a parallel of latitude but thinks it would have been the equator if it had its rights.'

Mark Twain.

CONVERSATION

'The talking is easy; it's the silences that are difficult.'

Author.

MARRIAGE

'There swims no goose so grey but soon or late, She finds some honest gander for her mate.' (An epigrammatic aphorism.)

Geoffrey Chaucer.

'A married man acquires a large vocabulary – by marrying it.'

Louie Ronson.

'A good marriage would be between a blind wife and a deaf husband.'

Montaigne (Essais, Book 3, ch. VI).

'A married man is a bachelor whose luck has failed him.'

Anonymous.

'Love is like war; you begin when you like and leave off when you can.'

Swanson Newsette.

'Stay single – and when your children grow up advise them to do the same!'

Cynic.

MAN

'Man is a creature who lives not upon bread alone, but principally by catchwords.'

Robert Louis Stevenson.

'He sows in a hurry and reaps indigestion.'

Robert Louis Stevenson.

'All the world is a little mad except you and me. And even you are a little mad.'

Old Saying.

VIEWPOINTS

'To know what we know, and know what we do not know, that is wisdom.'

Confucius.

'It is never unlucky to turn back if you are on the wrong road.'

Anonymous.

'Don't worry if you go bald. Just imagine if they ached and you have to have them out like teeth.'

Anonymous.

'What cannot be repaired is not to be regretted.'

Samuel Johnson.

'A gentleman considers what is right; the small man considers what will pay.'

Confucius.

'Humble because of knowledge; mighty by sacrifice.'

Rudyard Kipling.

'A classic is something by a dead Englishman or a live foreigner.'

Anonymous.

ASPECTS OF LIFE

'There are two things to aim at in life; first, to get what you want; and after that to enjoy it. Only the wisest of mankind achieve the second.'

Logan Pearsall Smith.

'I rather pride myself on knowing when to stand on my dignity and when to sit on it.'

>   *John Galsworthy (A Family Man, Act I).*

'I never saw such sad faces and such gay behinds.'

>   *Marshal Foch (after a visit to a Variety theatre).*

'There is only one rule about income. Make it first and make it last.'

>   *Anonymous.*

In reading through these examples I hope you will have found that some of them remain easily in the memory. Perhaps these are sayings which you will wish to use in conversation and with acknowledgement where this may be due.

If so, why not increase the number of sayings for yourself? Make your own compilation of aphorisms, noting down those which appeal to you personally or which seem to illustrate your views or to help dislodge the opinions you disagree with. Each time you hear or read a saying which appeals to you, jot it down. The more varied your list, the more useful it will be to you, ranging from 'A boy is an appetite inside a skin' to 'History repeats itself, but it puts the price up every time.'

In using your aphorisms be careful not to drag them in too often. Brief sayings should be used sparingly if they are to retain their effectiveness, and especially those which are thoughtful.

In conversation judicious use of aphorism makes unnecessary that long and laboured talking by which a point may be established or a meaning defined.

A good conversationalist will have available from his repertoire a story or saying which will briefly and clearly cut through the tangle of words and put his idea forward unmistakably and pleasantly. This means both that those who like to hear themselves talk can be kept in check and that the speaker's own view is sure of attention. Another advantage is that, at least in the earlier stages of your progress, the use of the brief sayings of others will not only help to teach you correctness of timing but will enable you to develop your own habit of brief utterance.

EASY START TO A CONVERSATION

We have already considered in great detail a method by which the difficulty of opening a conversation with one who is more or less a stranger may be overcome. Now we may add the advice that it is often useful to make your conversational approach by means of a short and striking saying.

For the conversationalist the use of aphorism guarantees to convey immediately to the person you address that your remark is not lightly made. If you have one or two remarks of topical interest, and possibly of different application, ready for the opening of a conversation you will find that your partner will respond to one of them, if not to the first. What you say is necessarily interesting and stimulating, *because* it is in the form of an aphorism. Consequently its qualities bring a reaction; the man you speak to will be impelled to reply, so that your opening now has the chance to grow into a conversation.

At the opening of this chapter it was stated that an aphorism is something confused with an epigram. This usage is now so frequent that it would be pedantic to insist on the distinction, at least in everyday speech. Nevertheless, we now look at the epigram properly so called in the original sense of the word. This meant 'a short poem', especially one containing a statement refined to conciseness. Connington's well-known translation of the epitaph ascribed to Simonides of Chios (d. 469 B.C.) is a good example:

'Go tell the Spartans, thou that passest by,
That here, obedient to their laws, we lie.'

Any saying so brief and metrical, and from which every unnecessary word has been excluded, is both easy to remember and incisive in use. The epigram is therefore an ideal means for expressing yourself clearly, pleasantly, and effectively. The same is true of most short jingles and we often use them in social life, as one who refuses cheese after lunch might murmur:

'Now cheese it is a peevish elf,
Digesting all things but itself.'

In conversation such verses are most useful and the epigram is the most useful of all, for its force comes at the end.

For material of this kind one must look to the famous epigrammatists or be alert to note down such epigrams as one may hear or come across in general reading of good literature. The poems of Alexander Pope abound in epigrams such as:

'In Faith and Hope the world will disagree,
But all mankind's concern is Charity.'

'On life's vast ocean diversely we sail,
Reason the card, but passion is the gale.'

'Avoid extremes; and shun the fault of such
Who still are pleased too little or too much.'

'Such laboured nothings, in so strange a style,
Amaze the unlearn'd and make the learned smile.'

'Some praise at morning what they blame at night,
    But always think the last opinion right.'

It would be possible to fill a small book with such epigrams from Pope, but we must leave him after a final quotation which has special value for conversationalists:

'Men must be taught as if you taught them not,
    And things unknown proposed as things forgot.'

The epigram is not necessarily as short as those above, as we see by a quotation from Winthrop Mack-Worth Praed's *The Vicar,*

'His talk was like a stream which runs
    With rapid change from rocks to roses;
It slipped from politics to puns:
    It passed from Mahomet to Moses.'

From the same author we may also select:

'And when religious sects ran mad,
    He held, in spite of all their learning,

That if man's belief is bad,
    It will not be improved by burning.'

A few more quotations may be found useful to start you off on your own collection.

'God bless the king, I mean the faith's defender;
God bless – no harm in blessing – the pretender;
Who that pretender is, and who is king,
God bless us all, that's quite another thing.'

John Byron.

'Swift flies each tale of laughter, shame, or folly,
    Caught by Paul Pry, and carried home to Dolly.'

Charles Sprague.

Aphorism and Epigram

'Oh, spare your idol! Think him human still;
Charms he may have, but he has frailties too;
Dote not too much, nor spoil what ye admire.'

William Cowper.

'Though man a thinking being is defined,
Few use the great prerogative of mind.
How few think justly of the thinking few!
How many never think, who think they do!'

Jane Taylor.

'Treason doth never prosper: what's the reason?
For if it prosper, none dare call it treason.'

Sir John Harrington.

'He slept beneath the moon,
He basked beneath the sun;
He lived a life of going-to-do,
And died with nothing done.'

James Albery.

'Time to me this truth has taught
    ('Tis a treasure worth revealing),
More offend from want of thought,
    Than from any want of feeling.'

Charles Swain.

I hope enough has now been written and illustrated to
make you feel at home in practising the use of aphorism and
epigram. Alertness of thought, crispness and originality of
expression, and freshness in use, are the main requisites.

8

THE USE OF GOOD STORIES

Most good conversationalists are also good *raconteurs*; they can almost always tell a story which is new, interesting, and, importantly, illuminating.

Whatever the topic of conversation, they can illustrate what they wish to say by putting it in story form. This has great value, for not only does everyone love a story but everyone remembers a story – and its point – better than a bare statement.

The ability to excel in this way depends on two things: the possession of a fund of good stories and the knowledge of how anecdotes should be told.

The first is easily obtained. Every week television, radio and magazines pour out hundreds of first-class stories most suitable for the conversationalist. Collections of stories useful to public speakers are valuable to the conversationalist. You are not necessarily looking for the belly-laugh or sex type of story, but for anecdotes, such as those taken from the sayings or actions of real people, which are capable of illustrating a point.

Amusing situations which have happened to you or your friends can be recalled again and again and, because of their personal angle, delight those listening but you must be sure never to slight anyone's character or cause hurt.

Examples of shrewd judgement make for good story telling but beware of blowing your own trumpet or you may get labelled a bighead! The principle or policy illuminated by such a story, as applied to the subject under discussion, will be more readily understood because it has been well presented.

Some people can reel off story after story, keeping us all thoroughly amused or otherwise entertained for a couple of hours. But 'useful yarns' are not exactly what you are looking for. What you require is a notebook *memorandum* of stories which either illustrate some point or are capable of being used as illustrations. That is to say, there must be in the tale a 'moral' which is arresting, apart from the humour or pathos of the story in itself. Each of the following stories stands by itself or may be used to exemplify a variety of ideas.

Some time ago a young man was committed by his family to a mental home. This greatly upset a wealthy friend of his, who immediately started spending a good deal of time and money to secure his release. After nearly two years of patient effort he succeeded in lining up three psychiatrists who testified that the young fellow was completely normal and always had been. The friend carried the doctors and the ex-patient off to his flat for dinner and celebration. Before the evening was over he asked, 'What are you going to do now? Go away for a holiday, I suppose, and then settle down as before.' 'Well, I thought of getting something to do, actually,' was the reply. 'Something quiet, of course, but interesting. Like writing a book. I have not really made up my mind whether to do that or take up painting again. On the other hand, of course, I might just go on being a tea-cosy.'

Stories about psychiatrists are innumerable and most of them remain current because there are so many quack 'psychologists' in practice, and because comparatively few people know what a psychiatrist actually does.

One amusing 'answer' to that question is best told in question and answer form: *Q*. 'What are the differences between psychologists, psychoanalysts and psychiatrists?' *A*. 'Psychologists build castles in the air, psychoanalysts live in them and psychiatrists, collect the rent!'

Tying in with a historical event is often a good way to introduce a joke while the subject is red hot. This story can be used every year around the time of July 4th when Americans celebrate their Declaration of Independence: 'At the beginning of the week coming up to July 4th a young high school teacher from Evanston, Illinois, hands every child in her class a special book all about their American heritage. Perhaps with a touch of inexperience she tells the children they will be having a test on the morning before the big day. The first question of her test after collecting in the books, is: "Who spoke the proclamation of the Second Continental Congress declaring that henceforth the thirteen American colonies would become politically independent of Great Britain and then signed it, and when did it all take place?" A subdued class said nothing. Then a faint voice ventured from the back in a Spanish accent "Was it John Hancock, Miss, in 1776?" "Well done, Miguel!" cried our teacher, "and as for the rest of you, you should be ashamed; here is young Miguel, who has only been in this class for six weeks since arriving from Mexico, and he seems to know more than all of you put together." There was a tense silence which was suddenly broken by an unashamed whisper ... "B...r the Mexicans!"

' "Who said that?" snapped the teacher. Quick as a flash came the full reply: "General Custer, at his last stand, battle of Bighorn, *1*876." '

With such a story, even if you are not good on the subject, make sure of your historical facts. It's worth the trouble and adds the punch a long joke needs. It also prevents a clever dick shooting you down half-way through.

Events sometimes provide the apt setting mirth requires. Waiting to cross a road with some friends one day, on our way to a restaurant, we none of us could help noticing a grossly fat, hideously dressed, ugly woman waddling along the pavement on the other side of the street. None of her clothes fitted her or toned in with each other. She stood out in focus because there were no other walkers on that side. The quip came from an otherwise quiet member of our party which somehow made it all the more side splitting. Without the need to point, all he said was: 'What a *glorious* outfit' ... then after a short pause while we mustered our attention ... 'Body, by Guchi!'

Here's one you might slip in after someone asks you for the correct time. A young gentleman in a hurry late one afternoon dives out of a Bond Street antique dealer's on to the pavement. He wants a taxi quickly. Over his shoulder, held like a gun at arms, is a magnificent grandfather clock. In the process of swinging round both ways looking for a cab the end of his clock strikes a fragile white-haired old man on the cheek, and knocks him clean off his feet. At that moment a taxi roars up. All the poor old chap had time to shout after the impatient young fellow was 'Can't you wear an ordinary wrist-watch like anyone else?!'

A little conversational ease among your working colleagues can carry you a long way up the ladder. This story apparently started life at a management training conference but it could add humour in many situations. 'The sort of fellow we want in our team,' said the speaker, 'must not just be involved; he must be *committed*.' He went on 'Let me explain by referring you to the great British breakfast, bacon and eggs. So far as the chicken is concerned in the production of this marvellous start to the day – well, she is involved I have to concede, but the pig, *he's* committed!'

From these examples you should be able to see the importance of the rule that an anecdote must have point in itself as well as a significance relating to the topic under discussion. A story should rarely be told, wholly for its own sake, however good it may be in itself, since alone it is merely entertaining. *If a story is told in conversation, it should link up with what has been said.*

Its point must be quickly seen – although there is the delayed action story which is most effective and requires expert telling – and should not require comment by way of explanation. If an explanatory remark is needed it should come before the story. This must be done, for example, if the point of the story depends on characterization; in this case, you should briefly make listeners familiar with the characters you are going to use.

WAIT UNTIL THE RIGHT MOMENT

Do not be in a hurry to tell your story as soon as it comes into your mind. Wait to choose the right moment. If the conversation takes an unforeseen rush beyond that point or veers abruptly off to another topic, do not interrupt to get the story in. To do this is to lose most of the effectiveness, because you are now drawing people's attention to something they have already considered, possibly inadequately, but that is irrelevant. The freshness has gone off the topic and you should be content to leave it alone. Keep your story for another day, which may come sooner than expected. Conversation often eddies round like a tide and comes back naturally to where it was earlier. If it does not do this, let the story go and reflect to see where your timing went wrong.

Sometimes, after a suitable gap, you can gently, skilfully, 'steer' the conversation back to your subject, ready to captivate the mood into which your joke is going to explode.

Timing is vitally important in the telling of jokes. One has to consider not only the right instant for introducing the joke but also the timing of the narration. Entertainers know that any jest will fail if its internal timing is faulty. If you want to learn the lesson well, pay attention to the telling of humorous stories on TV. Some jokes turn up fairly often, started by the experts and drifting thereafter through many degrees and alterations to the amateurs. The same jokes and quips of the top-liners become harassed, pale, over-worked, and creaky when reproduced by a second rate comic.

Even some of the most highly-paid comedians work up their stories and audiences by pitiful efforts like 'Talking of mermaids, I went down to Brighton the other day. Oh, yes, I went to Brighton ... lovely place ... very jolly ... Well, when I got to Brighton ...'

You must aim therefore to match the artistry of the really talented story-tellers who add each detail at exactly the right moment to cause the greatest effect, the whole scene building up till suddenly the punch line dissolves everyone into helpless laughter. Do not delay a story till it grows chilly, or hurry through it almost unnoticed.

EXPERIMENT ON FRIENDS

The right timing of a story can be acquired only by practical experience. There is nothing discouraging in this. It means that you should re-tell a story which appealed to you when told by an expert and notice if your narrative isn't as good as his. Try such a story on your friends. What goes wrong with it? Are you using too many words? Have you altered the exact position of the climax? Are you making too much of the details, perhaps making them so effective that the climax doesn't stand out sufficiently? Is your pace throughout too irregular, too slow, too rapid? By such questions you will surely master the timing which is so necessary.

Keep your story brief. Brevity has an effectiveness of its own which will go a long way towards making the story successful.

Your story should not normally depend for effect on anything which may be unfamiliar to your audience. One of the best stories I know is pointless unless you know the use of fracture boards. It is an excellent story to tell among doctors or nurses or people trained in first aid; in other company it requires a preliminary explanation, which unfortunately destroys the immediacy of the effect at the beginning.

Another way in which unfamiliarity may spoil effectiveness is found in those stories which depend on the oddity or originality or other personal quality of someone unknown to your listeners. Keep those stories for people who do know the character!

If, in the telling of a story, you find that some explanatory detail is needed, where you did not expect to be called on to supply it, try to slip in the information as if it were accidental. Put in a hesitation, perhaps, as if you had momentarily forgotten an item or couldn't recall a name. This is a very useful raconteur's trick if you notice that your audience is not *au fait* with what you are talking about. For example, even at the height of their fame, the most well known celebrities may yet remain unknown to your friends. Here is a story which shows how the method mentioned gets round any problem.

While he was taking a train journey in America, the famous scientist – er – the man who – er – worked out the theory of Relativity – er – Einstein, went to the dining-car, took up the menu, and found he had forgotten his glasses. Unable to read it, he handed it to the attendant and said,'I can't read it. Would you read it for me?' The man frowned at the card awhile, and then handed it back, saying, ' 'Fraid ah cain't. Ah'se ignorant, too, boss.'

MORE ADVANCED METHODS

By observation of the work of others and by your own self-criticism, you should be able to pass undeterred from short stories to those needing more skill. Your ability to indulge in some of the tricks of the trade will increase.

A quick opening may be followed by a leisurely sentence or two, seemingly almost irrelevant but actually calculated to heighten the climax to follow. These slower periods enable listeners to collect their wits, to pick up and appreciate the point given in the opening, and to see for themselves, without your having to waste words on it, a point which they will themselves link up with the climax, to its greater effect.

Your instinct for appreciating and telling a good story will grow through having a go and you will gain confidence as you find your judgement becoming more reliable.

Part of this development will have to come by rehearsal. A story *needs* rehearsal. The best story-tellers go over their best items repeatedly. The pause which comes pat at the right place, the tiny explanatory phrase slipped in unnoticeably, the hint of a smile which heightens suspense and indicates, 'It's coming now . . .' the sudden mimicry which makes a character come to life, all these and other aids occur so naturally that we may overlook the fact that they have been acquired by patient work. The raconteur may be such a master that he can do what he likes, telling every story with the knowledge that he will add every touch which it needs, in any company, but he was not always so expert. His eminence is due to the patient labour with which he laid its foundations. Like a trapeze artist or a conjurer he has prepared for months, maybe years.

When you converse you should be two people. One the person by whose knowledge and skill a real contribution is made to the conversation, the man who supplies the facts, the illustrations, the words. The other should be the critic, always alert, noting how the other man is faring, perhaps giving him a hint now and again, observing why he succeeds here or why he fails there. This is the man who has the ultimate enjoyment, for in every art there are two pleasures. One is the enjoyment of doing, of making, or using acquired skill. The other is the joy of noticing how this skill is succeeding in reaching its objective, or in analysing where, why and how it failed to do so. This isn't serious, unless we take ourselves too seriously about life itself. It is rather the all-embracing joy of a fun loving way of life.

9

MISCELLANEOUS METHODS
AND ETIQUETTE

The people who keep a conversation going are often those who continually feed in new facts and ideas. However, whether we are expected to talk about cabbages or kings, we must know of what we talk. We cannot know this unless we have a fund of facts in mind and with them suitable details, stories, examples and, perhaps, quotations from authorities.

To be 'at the ready' to enjoy yourself and join in with your contributions to any amusing company, needs to be an on-going process. It pays to plan a widely based repertoire of good general conversational topics. If you begin by focusing on just a few interests that excite *you*, it won't be long before you are master of enough knowledge to hold forth in conversation as long as you (or anyone!) may wish, whenever the opportunity arises.

By keeping to subjects *you* are keen about, you will automatically ensure that you will come over to your listeners enthusiastically enough to interest them. It will be easier for you to retain and recall points of fact which may reinforce your views.

People in groups, or at parties, etc., return to the same old subjects again and again. By having your views prepared on subjects you have observed are popular, much of the worry 'I haven't anything to say' will melt away.

Folk love to talk about films they have seen or books they

have read, for example. Rather than entertaining any tongue-tied feelings such as 'I wish I had seen that film too so I could talk about it' or 'How *do* they remember so much of that dull book?', try to concentrate on books or films *you did* enjoy. They hope you will be interested and pleased to hear what *they* enjoyed or dislike. Why not, therefore, extend them pleasure by reciprocating? Thus *you* will be *giving lively* interest to the conversation instead of dissipating energy despairing that you cannot hold your own in competition with others.

Keep in store, therefore, your views about a few films you have loved and several books you can recommend or talk about with delight. They will serve you well.

New advances in science may be another valuable field with which to hold people's attention. A regular glance at scientific journals will keep you up to date. Interest in such advances can come in useful when allied to a whole variety of possible talking subjects, from Agriculture to the meaning of Zen.

Keeping up with the daily news, both broadcast and printed, will repay many times over, the small sacrifice (if one can call it that!) of time it takes each day. The more you do it the easier it becomes to grasp key points and work them into your own views. Some areas of news are particularly useful and worth having topical information at hand upon.

For example, major sports like golf, horse racing or rugby. Then there are the Test Matches, Olympics or Wimbledon Tennis – plenty for everyone to find sporting interests of their choice. What the better known politicians are saying could be another situation to study, or perhaps the financial news would come higher on your list.

The main thing is to be selective – but in enough different

areas to give you something in common with plenty of different types of people. Being selective avoids the trap of trying to be all experts to all people and ending up being known for knowing nothing about anything!

While looking at ideas to feed the flow of contact among your friends it is worth memorizing a few neat expressions which can be slipped in for their amusement value. Examples can be found in use on TV, in the lovable language of Cockney Rhyming Slang, from the 'Slanguage' used on Citizen's Band radio in America, and from other such sources, and they will also be picked up from among your friends.

To quote just a few such deft expressions:

'A big girl's blouse' means a fool.

'The boob tube' stands for TV.

'The best thing since sliced bread' is a great new invention.

'Death's bladders' are bald tyres.

'Megabore' – extreme bore.

'Notes or rubber money' equals cash or cheque.

'Moral pigmy' person lacking courage of his true convictions.

'Hang a left' in driving means turn left.

Take care not to burden people with too many of these or to keep repeating them as they can become irksome to listen to!

At certain times when company meets, a spontaneous desire to sing funny songs will arise. There are always one or two who can supply the words and the lead. Only the effort to learn the tune and the verses are required for *you* to be one of those people! Be assured the rest of the company will be only too ready to join you in chorus, as everyone respects the effort *you* have made. Why not note down the lines of the next such song you hear which has great appeal?

Like songs, magic tricks, simple games and suchlike are useful to have up your sleeve on these occasions. The interest they attract is a great promoter of spontaneous conversation and you can make sure quieter people are thus automatically included in the fun whenever it is their turn.

Having given all these tips of the trade, I must add a note of caution. Lord Chesterfield, whose *Letters* contain several valuable lessons and observations about the art of conversation, sounds this apposite warning and it puts us on our guard against talking too much. This is a necessary advice for, when we know that we have many facts with which to support our conversation, we are in danger of overwhelming our companions with knowledge!

'I am far from meaning by this that one should always be talking wisely, in company of books, history and matters of knowledge. There are many companies which you will, and *ought* to keep, where such conversation would be misplaced and ill-timed; your own good sense must distinguish the company and the time. You must trifle only with triflers; and be serious only with the serious, but dance to those who pipe. From the moment that you are dressed to go out, pocket all your knowledge with your watch, and never pull it out unless desired: the producing of the one unasked implies that you are weary of the company; and the producing of the other unrequired will make the company weary of you. Company is a republic too jealous of its liberties to suffer a dictator even for a quarter of an hour; and yet in that, as in all republics, there are some few who really govern; but then it is by seeming to disclaim, instead of attempting to usurp, the power: that is the occasion in which manners, address and the undefinable *je ne sais quoi* triumph; if properly exerted, their conquest is sure, and the more lasting for not being perceived.'

Through understanding the wisdom of this advice, famous conversationalists know that they control talk as much by their silence as by their thoughtful and timely remarks.

AVOID BEING ASSERTIVE

Chesterfield's idea is that one should use the materials of conversation as one uses coins, in exchange for goods, buying here and there according to our judgements of the best markets. Before following him here, we may again protest against those talkers who imagine they are conversationalists because they do most of the talking.

Cowper remarked:

'Where men of judgement creep and feel their way,
 The positive pronounce without dismay.'
'Asseveration blustering in your face
 Makes contradiction such a hopeless case.'

People who talk emotionally but thoughtlessly often offend in this way, speaking at first from reason but on the least divergence of view, speaking with passion and heat, until all conversation dies either in a quarrel or in the desert of an endless monologue.

Remote from this is Chesterfield's idea of conversation, during which silences are used to foresee the effects of what is being said, to compare what is being expressed with what one thinks and in choosing the right time to put your own viewpoint reasonably, entertainingly if possible, and well.

During silence one should also be thinking of facts which may support the varying ideas of our companions. The purpose of this consideration is not to use them on one side or another. That would be insincere and fatally artificial. The aim in discovering and reflecting on such facts is to find out what may further stimulate the thought of others. You can ask the various speakers if this fact affects their opinion or this other fact any part of their conclusions. Leave these ideas to your companions to talk about, giving your own view whenever you wish. This is the way in which to handle the small change of conversation.

In making your contribution, give preference to those ideas which, as far as your knowledge of the group allows you to judge, will be of general interest. You know the interests of the people who are talking together; you know their habits of thought; you know their temperaments and natural inclinations. Make use of this knowledge as a guide in the handling of your ideas and reflections. Even if your knowledge of these things is incomplete, you can weigh the thoughts up as far as you may before deciding on what you will say yourself. This remark will probably arouse differences of opinion between A, B, and C. Do you want that? Now or later? Would it be better at this moment to stimulate a further exchange of ideas between these three before introducing the suggestion which may cause divergence? What can you do to widen the range of the conversation?

These are a few of the questions which may enter your mind as you attend to what is being said. What you offer need not only be a purposeful contribution to what is said; it can also help draw others into conversation between themselves.

For this purpose questions are eminently useful. They are stimulating, and, if carefully framed, lead to greater exactness of speech. Ask a speaker to define his meaning, to say exactly what he has in mind in using certain terms or phrases or how he may reconcile one fact with another. Ask for the production of facts in support of a statement.

In doing this be careful not to offend or to be inquisitorial. Inquisitive or impertinent questions are a sign of bad breeding and anyway, everyone notices people whose conversational technique consists of forever asking questions. The practice is bad, since it becomes apparent and then annoys. Moreover, it paralyses your own conversation. Yet once you know of it, it is useful on occasion and, at all times, it is amusing to notice how many men and women who are really of small attainment pass for highly successful conversationalists merely because they know this one method.

If questions are used unobtrusively and not too often their function as a conversational aid may be recommended. They have an occasional but not a regular value.

DON'T BE TOO WISE

Chesterfield had something to say about the less serious exchange of ideas and as usual he was helpful. He would not have us to be always talking too wisely nor too well. For this master of polite usage knew that it is often necessary or desirable that we should talk about the small events of life instead of about its profound problems. He did not wish us to confine ourselves to the lessons of history or the enigmas of human nature.

He recognized the value of talking 'nothings', and wrote, 'For in some companies it would be imprudent to talk of anything else; and with many people it is impossible to talk of anything else; they would not understand you.'

He returned to the point later and opened it out.

After referring to Descartes and Sir Isaac Newton, he declared:

'I honour and respect such superior geniuses; but I desire to converse with people of this world, who bring into company their share, at least, of cheerfulness, good breeding, and knowledge of mankind. In common life, one much oftener wants small money, and silver, than gold. Give me a man who has ready cash about him for present expenses; sixpences, shillings, half-crowns and crowns, which circulate easily: a man who has only an ingot of gold about him is much above common purposes, and his riches are not handy nor convenient. Have as much gold as you please in one pocket, but take care always to keep change in the other; for you will oftener have occasion for a shilling than for a guinea.'

SMALL TALK

Having conversational topics already prepared, therefore, should not preclude the use of comparatively small topics on suitable occasions. For instance, when members of a group are meeting for the first time, we should be able to secure their interest and promote an exchange of ideas by proposing several light subjects, acceptable to all and at the same time less dreary than 'the boredom of housework' or the cost of living.

Chesterfield writes, with reference to easy ways into general talking, 'There is a fashionable kind of small talk, which you should get; which, trifling as it is, is of use in mixed companies, and at table . . . where it keeps off certain serious subjects, that might create disputes or at least coldness for a time. Upon such occasions it is not amiss to know how to *parler cuisine*, or to be able to dissert upon the growth and flavour of wines. These, it is true, are very little things; but they are little things that occur very often . . .'

Such is the advice of a man of the world, who gave us the shrewd saying that, 'Where one would gain people, remember that nothing is little.'

In this connection I offer a suggestion which will be found useful. Have in readiness a few subjects which are slightly unusual or are in some way original. People whom we meet casually will find them refreshingly interesting and will therefore more readily enter into talk about them.

Subjects like campanology (church bell-ringing), how certain voluntary social services thrive, beekeeping, or any unusual hobby of your own are likely to be excellent topics. People will be intrigued to listen to your specialized knowledge. There's no need to keep it under a bushel! Take advantage of these assets in knowledge of yours.

10

ADVANCED CONVERSATIONAL CONCEPTS

What is it about a humorous story that makes peals of laughter a certainty? Success almost always derives, on my reckoning, from one kind or another of what is unfitting being said. It is the incongruity which bursts through our solemn guard. With appreciation of this you can learn to spot humour potential in the funniest places. I remember hearing a tale from a bartender which I have since dined out upon many a time. 'Years ago,' he opined, 'there were a dozen or so country gentlemen who used to come in on a Saturday night to this little bar. Each pulled out of his pocket all the cash he had (presumably that left over after handing his wife housekeeping money) and added it into one pile in front of me. The leading squire then rapped on top of the bar and said "O.K., barman," and after a pause, "take us away!"'

What is unexpected is usually amusing; this is one of our surest guides as to whether a story will succeed, as do the lines of the epitaph:

> This grave contains
> the last remains
> of little Ben, who spotted trains;
> all except the 6.02
> from Manchester Exchange
> to Crewe!

An ordinary story follows a straight line. While we listen to it we are all the time trying to anticipate the punch line. If there is an abrupt departure from the line we have been mentally forecasting, the fun in the story inevitably becomes firmly implanted in our minds. Here is an example of how such a joke is made to 'tick':

A guest was deep in conversation with his hostess when he was asked whether he would take more cabbage. He did not hear the question. When asked for the second time, he took a handful of cabbage from the dish and rubbed it slowly into his hair. He then resumed conversation until the hostess, astounded at what he had done, interrupted him by asking, 'Why did you rub the cabbage into your hair,' The man looked astonished. He stared about him and then said, 'I'm really sorry. To tell you the truth, I thought it was spinach.'

Being able to *show* your appreciation for the gift of another person's thoughts on subjects dear to you, is a vital part of the art of conversation. Great is the pleasure of acknowledging our gratefulness for thoughts given without expectation of reward. It is the sincerely meant thank you that forges strong trust and helps people, when they seek advice, to feel you can be *their* confidante. Always remember your thank you's.

When someone is emotionally upset they may be almost unable to talk to anyone, even to their closest friends or family. The need to expel their grief can reach a crisis level. With a special kind of listening patience, an understanding friend can work wonders. Someone who has reached uncontrollable tears may need a doctor but while waiting for his specialized help much can be done to dispel both your own, and perhaps your friend's, sense of alarm. By your drawing out the person's feelings into words expressed, he or she will begin to make sense of them. Bringing sad thoughts to the surface makes sure they stand the test of reason. Any unsound reasoning is thereby challenged and sensible thinking has the chance to dislodge sadness. The person's thoughts cease to go round and round in ever depressing circles.

A valuable first step is to assure the troubled soul that you will *not be* shocked whatever is the matter and that you are not going to try and force them to say anything they may not wish to. Add to this that you consider him or her to be *very* special, and so you have plenty of time to stay. If nothing is forthcoming from your friend make no attempt to steer the conversation. You will be better to just wait and see, perhaps adding an occasional remark to hold their confidence that you will not be running away. It may take minutes, or hours, before an attempt to talk comes. At first what is said may make no sense to you at all. But that doesn't matter. What matters is that *he or she* is coming to grips with whatever the problem is, not whether you can understand it. By listening and *going on* listening, without much more than an infrequent nod or gesture of the hand to show you are still attentive, the source of despair will unfold. Not necessarily completely in a few short hours but probably enough to restore calm, and then get the eyes dried with the return of at least a wan smile. Whatever you say, avoid implying any criticism or blame, no matter how much you may feel it appropriate. A person needs to come to see his faults, if indeed faults they are, *in his own way*. There will be time enough as days pass by for this to happen without you embroiling the sufferer in detailed arguments before he can possibly be ready to bring his mind to bear upon them. Meantime you will be able to consider objectively whether expert help may yet be needed.

The imperative need not to be critical or blaming can be

especially hard advice to follow when the person in deep trouble is in your close family or you are romantically involved. Steel yourself and control any such desire; it *will* be worthwhile in the end. When the whole episode has passed into history, and the sufferer has seen his misplaced thinking for what it was, if it was, would be time enough for criticism. By then your urge to insist on giving it will probably have long receded into the background, where it belongs. Over judgemental people frequently mask problems no less deep, of their own.

Having looked at ways to help specially sensitive or upset people brings me on to more common conversational blunders, traps into which unfortunately even well meaning people often fall. Do try not to interrupt shy friends when they *are* talking. Stronger people ride over interruptions using such ways as described on page 65 but an under-confident speaker, trying to express a complicated idea, can feel mortified by a cruelly placed slap down. Those wise in conversation reduce the ill-mannered interrupter in importance by paying little attention to him or reminding him of the good manners of letting another friend have *his* say. They recognize the blusterer who treads upon his acquaintances for what he is when he does, a bully.

Another nasty game spreads, so that you find yourself at it if you are not careful! It is the practice of picking fun of people in public; worse still it is if done behind their backs. When one of a party starts doing it the tendency is towards a verbal ping-pong match where each contestant merely tries to outdo the other. Others in the assembled company will be tempted to join in the fray. The game will continue every time the group meets and in the end even the ringleader will find his companions have just become bores. Wise conversationalists steer well clear of such frivolous people.

Another bad side-effect of this is it pushes shy people firmly aside into their shells. *Mistakenly* they think that they are foolish because they cannot stab with the 'skill' they see being thrown back and forth. *Instead* they should be glad they are *not* aiding or abetting such foul behaviour, misplaced aggression, masked by the cloak of superficial friendship.

If in a particular set of company you feel inferior, the chances are that you are wrong, completely wrong. You may be appalled by the thought of speaking to so many people at once, or you may be in the control of a bamboozler, or a manipulator. That is, one person who keeps putting you off.

To deal with the fear of commanding the attention of several people at once, or even a large public audience, you need to keep reminding yourself that the crowd is only after all, a collection of individuals, probably none more worthy than yourself. Looked at that way the problem dissolves into being no more difficult than talking to one person. Just as you appreciate hearing other people's views, which make them worthwhile people, so too are your opinions valuable *to them*. Without being proud or arrogant there is therefore *no reason* not to hold yourself and your ideas in the highest self-esteem.

If you find yourself constantly blaming yourself for not understanding or being clever enough to 'keep up', stop it. Apart from being so negative it can make you depressed! Yes, wonky thinking alone can cause depression. And it's a number one wrecker of conversational spontaneity. The best thing if you have been this way inclined is to count the number of times it happens in a day and to hit back into your great future by telling yourself, that number of times, that *really*, *you* are a *wonderful* person.

The first thing with a bamboozler or a manipulator, is to

identify him, to spot his methods for what they are. Then the fellow cannot ever again make you feel inferior. You can pull him up sharp whenever he tries to trespass on your feelings unfairly. Plainly, you can stand up to him.

For an example of a bamboozler I am grateful to *Esquire Magazine* of 488 Madison Avenue, New York, for permission to quote an article by Richard H. Rovere. He was commenting on Hitler and McCarthy:

'MULTIPLE LIES AND SHELL GAMES'

'He had an extraordinary bag of tricks. Hitler discovered the use of the Big Lie – the falsehood so large and round that reason, which deals in particulars, was almost powerless to combat it. McCarthy invented the Multiple Lie – the lie with so many particulars, so many moving and interchangeable parts, so many tiny gears and fragile connecting rods that reason exhausted itself in the effort to combat it. He said so many different things about so many different people (people, generally, of uncertain identity and even, so far as the public was concerned, of questionable existence) that no one could keep it all in focus.

'He brought to perfection a kind of shell game to be played with facts, or what George Orwell called "unfacts". He flummoxed me with it the first time I met him, which was a year or so before he discovered communism. I wished to get certain information about one of his undertakings, and he brought me into his office to show me some "documents" that would, he said, be TNT. "Wait'll you get a load of this," he said. "It's going to rock the country," All eager, I began to look at his photostats, his clippings, his "confidential" reports, his copies of other people's correspondence. A feeling of foolishness – mine, not his – came over me when I was unable to see that any of them proved anything about anything. No TNT. "But I don't quite get it," I would say. "It doesn't seem to have much to do with what I'm after." "It has a lot to do with it," he would say, "but naturally those bastards were trying to cover up. Now look at this one, it will make the others clear. We've got a jigsaw puzzle here, see, and we've got to put the pieces together," I thought he was making sense and that my perceptions were at fault, "Please explain this," I would ask, and he would answer, "It'll all be clear when you've studied a few more of these documents." He would deal some more from the bottom of the deck, and I would curse myself for my obtuseness. It was not until I had spent hours with him that it dawned on me that I was being switched, double-shuffled, and conned by one of the masters.'

The bamboozler has plenty more methods in his armoury all intended to make sure he gets his way. One trick he employs in debate is to bring in a lengthy red herring on the pretext that you must wait because it is relevant. It isn't and he knows so jolly well but he hopes you will have lost track of your thought train by the time he's through with it. Thus he is able to switch subjects and you suddenly find it's time to go home before your view has even been aired. One way to thwart his aim is to remind him that it is irritating and rude when people go off the point, and say that you will be pleased to hear his associated story later and judge its relevance then. This stand will certainly make him jump and probably lose his track as well, while you press home to the point of the discussion.

When a bamboozler sees he may be beaten he will often fall back on meaningless observations designed to make you feel guilty for opening your mouth. Common such assertions are 'Listen to the voice of experience'; 'You shouldn't try to teach your grandfather to suck eggs'; 'Rubbish!'; 'Everyone knows it's true; it's well known'; these are all about as unfair to use in debate as the 'because Mummy says so' which a mother may rely on to explain things away to her child; they are the shield behind which the bamboozler tries to hide his ignorance or defend some misplaced pride in never being proved wrong. Bamboozlers are often so used to getting away with it, the technique becomes almost unconscious for them.

Though it may seem painful to stand up to them at the time because they belittle your stand, you can rest assured you will have made them think. Their respect for you will in reality be much enhanced every time it happens (provided you are not merely being stubborn for the sake of stubbornness, i.e. you are sure of your ground). Their habit of bamboozling will soon cease where you are concerned. The boot will be on the other foot in future, with them being wary as to how they back up their views, instead of you.

The manipulator is rather more insidious than the plain bamboozler. His campaigns are subtle and often long lasting. His aim is not only to win in conversation; he wants to control your actions as well. Under the guise of being your friend he wants to use you. Again he is very likely to be unconscious of this game he plays.

Directly you make clear that you won't 'buy' his grasp you will find his tentacles move elsewhere. In its worst but perhaps most obvious form his method may resort to emotional blackmail. 'You've got to help me; I can't live without you' and similar nonsense.

At a more subtle level you find the manipulator demands an excessive amount of your time. He invites you to his home not so much to offer the gift of friendship to you, as to boost his low ego. To prove to the neighbours or other guests that he has such nice friends as you. Or it may be that he fears ever being on his own and so he wants a constant stream of visitors. We all know such apparently hospitable people and they are hard to detect from those of genuine goodwill.

A good test is to ask them along to do things *you* want to do instead, and see just how interested they are prepared to be in being included in your wishes or plans. Stay away from their company rather more than usual on this basis, and you will soon find out whether their interest is purely selfish or not – if they will now do as much for you as you were doing for them. This is the way to free yourself from feeling guilty for not agreeing to so many of their selfish needs. They want you to feel guilty, so you are pushed into going along with them all the more.

Within the family or a romance beware of the manipulator, lurking so close he remains unseen. And remember that because someone attempts to control you in one or two ways doesn't make him an ogre in all other ways. No doubt you are guilty yourself on one or two counts. So there's no place for anger or blame or making over severe judgements. Firmness is all that's required.

The clinging type of hanging on which can enter the home or the love life can be very painful and may need much courage to rout out. But cleared the air must be for if matters are not allowed to prey on the mind, unspoken, conversation between those who are close can be suffocated. Ugly rows and rifts are the likely end result. A return to proper rapport may be hard indeed but it stands little chance until the attempts at control are shown up for what they are. Then the bothersome business can be dealt with with the backing of fair play. Once the controller has been faced with the truth of his game he can be checked. Every time he is picked up over his sense of fair play, will make him easier to discuss with in the future, as he can be reminded that that game doesn't work.

Once you are sure you have been or are being manipulated, and that you are not merely being over-sensitive, you can easily dispel the almost hypnotic effect such a person can have upon you. No longer do you need to be drawn into his or her cleverly spun net, as is the fly by the spider. A firm stand sets you free. Moreover it proves to you that any guilt or inferiority you may have been feeling under his or her spell was wrong, completely wrong.

As an example of this sort of manipulation we can look at the parent–child relationship at the time the offspring are ready to break free of the nest. In the normal way parents remain fairly neutral or encouraging about their son's or daughter's desires to leave the home. If the children remain longer than perhaps the majority of their friends in the locality have done a few hints may be given, or a suggestion or two of things to do that would automatically involve going away. By contrast the manipulative parent may try to hold on to the youngster by pointing out how cheap it is to stay home, insisting how nice it is here and any of a whole host of, at first glimpse, friendly devices. Their remarks tend to be capped with emotionally muddling daggers such as: 'We love you so much, darling; surely you know we are only trying to help by suggesting the best thing for you,' etc., etc. In cold print such remarks can be seen for the patronizing and neurotic tricks they are. Unfortunately in the heat of a typical family situation they can inflict lasting damage.

There is an area of 'conversation' not so far mentioned, namely that of facial expressions, hand gestures and other movements of the body. Overdone they can annoy but it is possible to cultivate a few amusing and welcoming ways to add polish to the way in which you deliver your words. If you lack the cheerful illustrative mannerisms that you notice among your successful conversational friends, perhaps it is time to develop a style of your own. Giving your personality the airing it deserves! That methods you may develop may be an amalgam of others you have observed does not matter, unless it is too obvious you have copied only one person nearly everyone in your circles happens to know.

Inventions and discoveries generally only come about when the last piece of the jigsaw is found to fit. The inventor or discoverer has been largely dependent upon information already widely known; his accolade is for finding the final part that counts in making it and all the others together form a new conclusion. Thus it would be silly to expect yourself to come out with gestures entirely new. You can be content and pleased with ones merely adapted for your own use or used in entirely different circumstances.

Using a telephone well is another conversational skill worth development. A chatty, cheerful snappy opening can work wonders and set the tone for fruitful exchange between the parties. A dull monotonous opening or an abrupt 'helloh' at the other end may have the reverse effect. A little carefully chosen flattery in your opening, if done occasionally, rarely goes amiss, for example, to someone you know is a keen yachtsman, you could open with 'May I speak to Admiral so and so please?' In business when you know the people at the other end well, you might get away with 'Is the big chief there today?' You can pick up little ways which will help the person you call to recognize you instantly by observing which other callers' mannerisms stick in your memory.

Everybody loses track of what they were saying sometimes, especially over the phone. A good ploy when this happens is to say 'whoops, my mind's gone into neutral again!' and carry on with your next topic while waiting for the earlier one to return to you. The truthful self-acceptance of the problem you have thereby shown, encourages your waiting listener to have patience. Usually the hint of humour distracts you sufficiently from self-annoyance to make sure you do remember!

To break a long and difficult silence is sometimes hard. One way tried on me by a friend once used my sense of fun to crack the silence. He simply cut in with 'I'm sorry; where were we? I must have fallen asleep!'

Not many conversational methods are peculiar to the telephone but one last one is worth a mention. It is the unexpected 'Good-bye!' The technique is used by the initiator of the call to emphasize his main point doubly. It is a rather one-sided thing to do because the abruptness with which he cuts off the call just when you were about to speak leaves you no chance to ask a question or put a viewpoint! What it does do is to bring into sharp relief for you the message he put across. You cannot but help think back through the conversation to make sure you did understand the point, as you listen to the burr of the now dead line. An example will illustrate: 'John, as an insurance man you should see this! It's an article from our parish magazine this month about the small print on insurance policies; I expect you have a copy or can easily get one. I heard Charlie and Jim talking about it at dinner, got involved and decided to give it a quiet read when I got home. As they said it is a brilliant analysis. Actually, as soon as I heard them going on about it I knew, that because we both agree they are pretty bright chaps, you would also be interested – so I pricked up my ears! Good-bye!' click, burr-rr-rr-r, etc. The caller whetted John's appetite enough to make sure he would dig out the article but cut off before finding himself having to waste time explaining all the minutiae of detail. It was a friendly gesture concisely pressed forward, which didn't need to go any further. John, having read the article, was able to thank his friend and comment on it the next time he saw him, when time was not so precious.

END

The author recommends for further reading:
To anyone who find themselves depressed by apparent inability in conversation and that these sad defeated feelings seem to be the hardest hurdle to jump – *Overcoming Depression* by Paul Hauck, published by Sheldon Press SPCK, Marylebone Road, London NW1 4DU, England.

The book combines commonsense psychology with sound explanation of how religion and psychology in fact support and agree with each other on vital issues.

TAILPIECE

The author welcomes readers' questions (and constructive criticisms). If you write care of Elliot Right Way Books, Kingswood, Surrey, U.K., he will be pleased to try and be of further help. Please enclose a stamped addressed envelope.

OTHER GREAT PAPERFRONT BOOKS

Each uniform with this book

PERSUASIVE SPEAKING

Uniquely designed to emphasize and explain the author's eleven principles of persuasive speaking. The art and science of persuasion depends on emotional speaking. W. George Jehan shows how to do it.

SAMPLE SOCIAL SPEECHES

This brilliant ready-to-use technique is based on numerous specimen speeches and enables you to build up your own social speech for any occasion. Gives many sample speeches to which you can add with gay or serious stories from this unique collection.

THE RIGHT JOKE FOR THE RIGHT OCCASION

Everyone can reduce their friends to helpless peals, ripples, tickles, bubbles, squeaks, hoots and tears of laughter with this joke directory. There is no need to be left out or tongue-tied if you dig into this mine of humour.

FACE THAT INTERVIEW

Sets out in a logical sequence the essential preparations for an interview to ensure that you are the applicant selected for the job. Here's how to acquire the know-how and confidence you need.

YOUR BUSINESS, THE RIGHT WAY TO RUN IT

Comprehensive and Instructive. Details most aspects of business learned in 45 years in home and export markets. Organization, premises, equipment, money and systems, tax, personnel, legal aspects, costing, pricing, sales, publicity, goodwill, insurance, etc., are all covered.

THE RIGHT WAY TO SPEAK IN PUBLIC

Never before has any writer gone so deeply and clearly into the subject. The reader who attends carefully to the instructions can, if of at least average ability, acquire the knowledge which will enable him to captivate an audience and hold it spellbound.

THE HOME MEDICAL ENCYCLOPEDIA

All illnesses and medical terms appear in A–Z order for simple reference. The easy-to-understand way in which this complex book is written is a triumph, and the book is free of medical phrases unfamiliar to the layman.

ELECTRONIC CALCULATOR

Designed to disentangle the problems which perplex a wide range of people. Businessmen, householders, students and school pupils – all will increase their understanding of the straightforward principles which lie behind operations possible on the calculator.

CAR DRIVING IN TWO WEEKS

26th edition of this Learner's 'Bible' completely re-written, based on the Highway Code, with a brilliant Q & A section to help you sail through your test. Money back guarantee if you fail.

GENERAL AND SOCIAL LETTER WRITING

If you find any difficulty in letter writing you need this book. Tells you how to write letters and make them interesting. Packed with samples.

THE RIGHT WAY TO IMPROVE YOUR ENGLISH

A gaily written explanation of the errors into which the beginner and experienced can so easily fall. The contents will lead to a thorough command of English and help you to progress in all walks of life.

BUSINESS LETTERS, CONTRACTS AND ETIQUETTE

This is a specialized companion volume which covers Contracts and Etiquette. Chapters include: 'Elementary Grammar, Construction and Punctuation', 'Style and Construction'. 'The Risks of Letter Writing', 'Publicity and Sales Letters', 'Forms of Address and Subscription', etc.

All uniform with this book

This is only a small selection from the wide range of *Paperfronts*. A full catalogue can be had FREE by sending S.A.E. to the address below.

ELLIOT RIGHTWAY BOOKS
KINGSWOOD, SURREY, U.K.